T0317100

GIVE THE BEST AWAY

ROSEMARY LANCASTER MBE

WITH

MURRAY WATTS

MONARCH
BOOKS

Oxford UK, and Grand Rapids, USA

Text copyright © 2016 Rosemary Lancaster and Murray Watts
This edition copyright © 2016 Lion Hudson

The right of Rosemary Lancaster and Murray Watts to be identified as the authors of this work has been asserted by them in accordance with the Copyright, Designs and Patents Act 1988.

All rights reserved. No part of this publication may be reproduced or transmitted in any form or by any means, electronic or mechanical, including photocopy, recording, or any information storage and retrieval system, without permission in writing from the publisher.

Published by Monarch Books
an imprint of
Lion Hudson plc
Wilkinson House, Jordan Hill Road,
Oxford OX2 8DR, England
Email: monarch@lionhudson.com
www.lionhudson.com/monarch

ISBN 978 0 85721 814 8
e-ISBN 978 0 85721 816 2

First edition 2016

Acknowledgments
Scripture quotations marked "NIV" are taken from the Holy Bible, New International Version Anglicised Copyright © 1979, 1984, 2011 Biblica, formerly International Bible Society. Used by permission of Hodder & Stoughton Ltd, an Hachette UK company. All rights reserved. "NIV" is a registered trademark of Biblica. UK trademark number 1448790.
Scripture quotations marked "KJV" are taken from the Authorized (King James) Version: rights in the Authorized Version in the United Kingdom are vested in the Crown. Reproduced by permission of the Crown's patentee, Cambridge University Press.
Scripture quotations marked "NKJV" are taken from the New King James Version®. Copyright © 1982 by Thomas Nelson. Used by permission. All rights reserved.
Scripture quotations marked "ESV" are taken from The ESV® Bible (The Holy Bible, English Standard Version®), copyright © 2001 by Crossway. Used by permission. All rights reserved.
Scripture quotations marked "The Message" are taken from THE MESSAGE, copyright © 1993, 1994, 1995, 1996, 2000, 2001, 2002. Used by permission of NavPress Publishing Group.
Extract p. 59 taken from *Superstar*. Music by Andrew Lloyd Webber. Lyrics by Tim Rice. © Copyright 1970 MCA Music Limited. Universal/MCA Music Limited. All Rights Reserved. International Copyright Secured. Used by permission of Music Sales Limited.

Every effort has been made to trace copyright holders and to obtain permission for the use of copyright material. The publisher apologizes for any errors or omissions and would be grateful to be notified of any corrections that should be incorporated in future reprints of this book.

A catalogue record for this book is available from the British Library

Printed and bound in the UK, October 2016, LH29

DEDICATED TO

Josh, Maddie, Erin, Tilly, Levi, Gracie, and Soli.
Thank you
for keeping me forever young.

"Those close to Rosemary know that she is an unassuming, gentle lady who shuns the limelight. To go public with her story is a remarkable act of courage. Thrust onto a stage she never sought, through the success of her husband's business, Rosemary puts into practice what she learnt from her mother, 'to give the best bits away'. This book tells the amazing story of lives changed because of doing just that. It is told with warmth, honesty, compassion and humour; traits that Rosemary has in abundance. I am glad that this book has become more than just a 'letter' to her grandchildren. It is about extraordinary events but it is also about an extraordinary lady."

Reverend Mark Pickett

Contents

Acknowledgments

I would like to thank my dear friend Jilly Farthing, who has been a constant encouragement to me: she has helped me to keep courage throughout the writing of this book. Thank you also to my friend Murray Watts, who has been my faithful guide and companion in recent years, helping me to craft my story.

A very special thank-you to my family: Steve and Anna, Julie and Phil, and to all my grandchildren, Josh, Maddie, Tilly, Levi, Erin, Gracie, and Soli – this book is my gift to them and has been inspired all the way by their love and their hopes and dreams. Thank you to my dear sister, Lynne, for always being there – from the beginning! – and to her dear husband, Keith, and not least to my great-niece, our "miracle baby", Lili Rose Whittaker, who has reminded me so often that nothing is impossible…

Bob and Debby Gass have offered constant inspiration, blessing, and encouragement through UCB and *Word for Today* – I have needed such wisdom in my life. Thank you.

I would like to thank Tony Collins very much, our editor at Lion Hudson, who has really believed in this book and helped to make this publication possible at last.

My husband, John, is a character throughout this book – and the main character in my life! Thank you for everything: the love, the friendship, the fun, the roller coaster of experience and for being my best buddy and soul mate… Love you xx. Although, I have to admit, there is now one little character who is a near-rival, Megs the dog! Her mischief and energy and affection have kept me going day by day.

Finally, I have to mention all those names that are written on my heart and are mentioned in this book, and who are held, as I am, in the embrace of the One whose name is Love – to whom "all thanks and praise are due".

Megs, our dog

View from La Bénédiction.

Prologue

**"Faith is the bird that feels the light and sings
when the dawn is still dark"**

Rabindranath Tagore

January, 2010… This is such a peaceful place to be, our beautiful holiday home in the Swiss mountains, La Bénédiction.

My husband, John, is still sleeping, a pleasant luxury at our age. Gone are those days of business demands – tight schedules have become a very distant memory.

Morning is my favourite time of day: a time to reflect, to pray, to just be me. Snow is softly falling; the majestic mountains are hidden from view behind a veil of mist. A lone bird sings to the dawn, announcing the mysterious moment when all will be revealed.

And darkness was upon the face of the deep…

Genesis 1:2 (KJV)

In the Dark Ages there was a village in England called Clitherhow, meaning "the rock by the river". Five hundred people lived there and struggled to survive. By the year 2000, thanks to the cotton mills of the nineteenth century and the march of progress throughout the twentieth, the population of the place now spelled Clitheroe had increased to 14,000. But, in different ways, the twenty-first-century people of this small town still struggle to survive.

This is where I was born and have lived all my life, and this is the place where John and I have gone through darkness and light, and light and darkness. This is the small town, the rock beside the river, where the bird of faith has been singing for us.

I hope it will sing for you as I tell you my story. With all its ups and downs, it is a story that is well told in a place called La Bénédiction. I have been touched, once again, by all the memories and reflections, and I have been filled with gratitude, even as I have laboured over this for longer than I planned. Six years ago I simply set out to write a very long letter to my grandchildren! I just wanted so much to share my life and experiences of God's grace with them. But, gradually, the project grew and I began to realize that this story of blessing was not just for our little family, but hopefully for many people around the world.

CHAPTER ONE

Floating!

It is 17 October 1997. A day that burns in my memory, because it would change my life for ever – and the lives of hundreds of thousands of people around the world.

A taxi is whizzing round the City of London, racing from one pension fund to another, from one bank to another, from one financial institution to another.

My husband, John Lancaster, entrepreneur, founder, and CEO of Ultraframe, is grinning crazily with delight as he hurtles through the greatest financial centre of the world. He can't help visualizing his younger self, the lad who left school in Clitheroe at the age of fifteen, with no qualifications and no prospects. "Nothing will come of your life" – the harsh words of his teachers still echo in his mind.

"Nothing will come of you! No good! Failure!"

But John is laughing with glee as the taxi gathers speed. He is beginning to feel like a Formula One racing driver heading for the chequered flag. He now knows that this is no dream or fantasy. This is truly his day.

Everywhere he goes, every door he opens, every executive he greets confirms the amazing reality that is unfolding…

Ultraframe is being admitted to the London Stock Exchange with "an initial market capitalization" of… £136 million.

I am in Clitheroe at the factory. John telephones me from London with the flotation share price, and I am in such shock that I get everything wrong as I relay the information to the puzzled employees.

"It's £136,000," I mumble.

"No, no!" John is hollering on the phone. "*Millions*. It's bloomin' millions, Rose! One hundred and thirty-six million pounds!"

The place goes wild. People are shouting, cheering, laughing, dancing… they soon have their paper and pencils out to do some calculations. On average, our workforce makes £20,000 each on this day… and, in a very short time, this amount has doubled and tripled.

The truth is, we gave away £13 million to our employees on 17 October 1997, because we felt very deeply that this was what God had called us to do. He had blessed us beyond our wildest dreams, but He hadn't blessed us for our own sake. And we knew now that He had a purpose behind this staggering windfall that was meant to bring healing, hope, and joy to many people. In the very instant of our astonishing good fortune, we knew that a profound responsibility had come to us, and, in many ways, the story of our lives as they had moved through poverty, hardship, and some extreme circumstances had prepared us for this.

But, to set the scene, I need to roll back the clock some eighty years…

CHAPTER TWO
Family History

You may have read about "the Great Depression" in history books. You may have heard of a time when the whole world was in terrible financial trouble. Everywhere businesses went bankrupt, people lost their jobs, lives were ruined, whole countries were facing impossible debts. Apart from the great wars of the twentieth century, this was one of the most desperate times in human history – but the Great Depression was not history to my parents. It was their life.

My mum and dad were married in 1935. The wonderful happiness of their wedding day was like a shaft of sunshine in a very dark world. The Great Depression was casting a long shadow over their home town. Clitheroe's economy was in crisis, with unemployment rising to 80 per cent. People were starving, and the threat of going to the workhouse terrified young married couples. The workhouse was not a faint memory, belonging to the world of Charles Dickens novels and TV dramas; it was down the street in Chatburn Road. It was very real and frightening in 1935 – a grey, forbidding building betokening utter shame and desolation. The mere sight of the workhouse would send

Lily and Jim Cook, Rosemary's parents.

a shudder down the spine of any young couple passing by who were facing extreme poverty, because it was the place where people were sent when they had nothing: no money, no food, and no future. For many, it was a sentence of death.

Today, we think of tramps and homeless people going to soup kitchens and sleeping on park benches; we think of children in Ethiopia or the Sudan suffering from starvation and disease, but across Britain in the 1930s thousands of families were left destitute. Queuing at soup kitchens became a way of life for many ordinary and hard-working people.

The horrors of malnutrition, rickets, and tuberculosis were rife. My parents, Jim and Lily Cook, struggled to survive in a very hostile world.

Quite apart from the daily battle to obtain food and clothing, Jim and Lily had many other trials too. They had managed to rent a small house in what was known as a poor area of Clitheroe. My dad worked as a builder's labourer and my mum stayed at home, happy to wait for their new baby. Their joy quickly turned to heartbreak when, following a very difficult delivery, their beautiful baby, Sylvia – my elder sister – survived for only a few minutes at St Mary's Hospital in Manchester. My dad silently placed her tiny body in a shoebox. He said goodbye to Mum, fighting back tears and hiding his emotions. He carried his lifeless daughter back home, a gruelling thirty-six miles by bus. He could never bring himself to talk of that terrible day. He wouldn't tell Mum where he had buried her body. Mum guessed that their little one had been laid in a communal grave, a special area reserved for stillborn babies.

I was walking with her through Clitheroe Cemetery many years later, when Mum pointed out to me a small area under a tree.

"I think that's where your dad buried Sylvia," she said, and her eyes told me everything I needed to know of the sorrow that was buried even deeper.

Happily, in 1937, another baby was born. He was a joyful, bouncing boy called James. He was certainly a ray of hope in their troubled lives, and his happy little character must have given them strength as the whole world slowly descended into the darkness that we now call the Second World War. If the Great Depression had nearly broken the spirit of many people in Britain, the war brought the country together in a remarkable way. The deadly threat brought out great virtues of bravery and endurance and my parents were no exception to this, although the war took an unexpected toll on their lives. It was to leave our family scarred and heartbroken, like so many others.

Lily Cook with James.

On 3 September 1939, Neville Chamberlain, First Lord of the Admiralty, addressed the nation at 11.15 a.m. on the BBC Radio Home Service:

> *… I have to tell you now that no such undertaking has been received, and that consequently this country is at war with Germany… We have a clear conscience. We have done all that any country could do to establish peace. The situation in which no word given by Germany's ruler could be trusted and no people or country could feel themselves safe has become intolerable… Now may God bless you all. May He defend the right. It is the evil things that we shall be fighting against – brute force, bad faith, injustice, oppression and persecution – and against them I am certain that the right will prevail.*

Dad enlisted for active service, training as a rear gunner in the Royal Air Force. Meanwhile, Mum faced the loss of her job as a winder when the cotton mill closed because there was neither enough cotton nor enough workers to continue – but she was determined to play her part too. The limestone around Clitheroe was exceptionally good for making cement and so Mum found employment hand-sewing cement bags, working long and laborious hours, yet never complaining. She was simply thankful to be well employed in the war effort and to be providing for her precious little boy, James. She paid a price for her dedication, however. She developed industrial dermatitis, which was an extremely painful skin disorder that covered her arms and hands. She endured this condition for many years. I remember feeling terrified as she would remove the dressings to reveal raw, weeping flesh and flaking skin. She always suffered silently, doing whatever she could to ease the discomfort.

Dad trained hard in the RAF, preparing for active service, desperately wanting to join all those brave young men on the front line. Unfortunately, his health began to deteriorate as a result of painful kidney stones. The doctor declared him "Unfit for Armed Service". This was a devastating blow to any Englishman in 1940. It may be the case today, in a world of confused and often pointless wars, that someone might rejoice at escaping from active service (I remember how, in the Vietnam War of the 1960s and 1970s, many young men tried to get out of military service and became known as "draft dodgers"), but the world was very different in 1940. And few doubted then (or doubt today) the horrible evil that was perpetrated by Adolf Hitler and the Nazis. The whole of Britain – men, women, and children – was at war together against one of the greatest threats to humanity the world has ever seen. Of course, there were a few "conscientious objectors" and "pacifists" who refused to fight, but they were all involved in contributing to the war effort, unless they preferred to go to jail. My dad, Jim Cook, was determined to fight. For him, it was a matter of honour, and deeply important to him. So when he was rejected, he was inconsolable.

He underwent surgery in a military hospital to remove one of his kidneys and was then sent home to recuperate. But he was never considered "Fit for Active Service". He would suffer poor health throughout his entire life. He was always stoical, uncomplaining, and "tough as old boots". I have no doubt that he would have made a great wartime fighter, but instead he fought the odds stacked against him all his life – he was a true warrior. He really did have a strong constitution, with amazing willpower. Despite his disabilities, he did odd jobs in order to provide for his family, with that great sense of pride that Lancashire folk are known for. He never wanted to be a burden to anybody and the thought of going through a means test for state benefits – seen as begging for handouts – was abhorrent. "If tha had two hands to work wi', then tha mon use 'em," he would say.

Eventually, Dad found regular work as a gamekeeper on an estate at Sawley, an idyllic village five miles east of Clitheroe. A small terraced cottage came with the job, so Mum and my brother James moved to a life in the country.

James was a truly happy child and loved their small garden. He delighted in picking the flower heads and presenting them to Mum, who was always pleased and managed not to scold him for picking too many! He had such a winning smile that it was impossible to be cross with him. Mum and Dad adored him, and I suppose this very brief period of their life, in the midst of a war-torn world, was like a glorious oasis. Their own paradise in a Lancashire village.

Meanwhile, London was blitzed nightly. The government decided to evacuate all the children to safe locations. Nearly 300 children were sent to Clitheroe from London. No one could have guessed the huge and fateful impact this would have on my family.

My gran had a young evacuee staying with her. Naturally, my mum would leave little James with her mother during working hours. She knew he would be safe and secure and could enjoy the friendship of another little boy, playing and laughing together. It seemed a perfect situation, but the quiet domestic scene concealed an invisible threat just as lethal as any German bomb. The boy from London had diphtheria. James caught the disease, dying slowly of asphyxiation.

Just before he died in Mum's arms, he gazed outside and whispered, "Who's that at the window?"

Tears streaming down her face, she replied, "That's your guardian angel watching over you." Who knows what he saw, as he lay struggling to breathe, his tiny throat gradually closing… rasping, rasping… then silence.

Thick darkness descended over my parents' lives once

again. Their precious only son was gone. Their one little light had been snuffed out.

The death of one child is painful enough, but two... how do you come to terms with a double tragedy? My mum did not come to terms with it.

Every day, she walked to Clitheroe Cemetery. She knelt down beside his fresh grave. She was stricken with grief and began to think about ending her own life.

Far below the cemetery, on the east side of Coe Hill, the River Ribble meandered along peacefully... but, one day, the shining snake of water reminded her of a dreadful old folk tale. In the seventeenth century, a young maidservant at Waddow Hall had fallen in love with the eldest son of the

James, aged 4.

squire, but the lady of the manor cast the maidservant out in her fury. It was unthinkable that a working-class girl should marry the son of the gentry! Days later, Peg O'Nell's body was discovered drowned. Some said she was murdered but all agreed that she had uttered a curse before her death: every seven years, someone else would drown in the River Ribble.

My mum walked slowly down towards the weir near Waddow Hall, the curse of Peg O'Nell drawing her towards the water. All she could think of was finding peace from her endless torment: "No more pain, just peace…" Remarkably, at that very moment, she met her midwife, who asked her gently, "How are you doing, Lily?" My mum poured out all her sadness, weeping desperately for the child she had lost – and seemed to lose over and over again, every single day.

"Lily," said the midwife softly, "let James go. You're not helping him, yourself, or your husband by holding on." Those words, spoken in love, helped my mum finally to come to terms with her tragic bereavement.

The following year Lily and Jim Cook had another child, a beautiful little girl called Lynne, born on 8 May 1942 – in the year that many said was Britain's darkest hour. But, for my parents, in the midst of a world torn apart, where hope and civilization were in the balance, a bright new light was shining. The birth of Lynne helped them to face many hard challenges. My dad's health was deteriorating and he had to leave his job as a gamekeeper, and so they lost the lovely tied cottage in the country and returned to Clitheroe. There, they rented number 14 Monk Street, a mid-terrace, two-up, two-down house. The property had cold flagstone floors, coal fires for heating, no bathroom, and a tippler toilet in the yard. The kitchen-cum-living room was infested with cockroaches and mice, compliments of the flour mill and abattoir operating at the end of the street. Yet my mum was immensely proud of her little home.

Hope is one of the greatest gifts we can have in the midst of all our troubles, and I believe that this was a very special kind of new start for my mum. A healthy new baby… a new home… even in the context of a war-torn world, this was a dream coming true. The truth is that my mum had a very deep need for security and for a strong sense of family, because there was a dark secret in her past. She had been born illegitimate and in those days there was a deep shame associated with such an unpromising beginning to life. Incredibly, my father shared the same heritage: he too had been born illegitimate. I only discovered this in later life, and I felt a little like those people who explore their family history on the popular TV series *Who Do You Think You Are?* I began to wonder, "Who do I think I am?", but, in the midst of all the emotion, I came to appreciate how my mother especially had created such a strong future for our family, against all the odds. She was a real heroine, a true survivor.

One thing my parents had in abundance, despite their hardships and poverty, was family, friends, and neighbours all looking out for each other. In the bleak world of wartime Clitheroe, with its cramped little streets and food rationing, my parents had an amazing wealth of love and support. It's almost impossible to explain to anyone the contradictions of that time, when people had nothing compared with the modern world, and yet had everything.

13 July 1945. A cry in the night... a new life... the agony of childbirth forgotten. Mum is holding me in her arms, beaming with pride. Joy and hope for the future are ringing out from that first little cry.

"We'll call her Rosemary. Rose after the flower of England; Mary after Queen Mary!"

Peace is announced: there are street parties and wild celebrations across the country. Britain will be great once again!

It's a curious fact that the older you get, the brighter and more vivid the memories of childhood become – perhaps one day these memories will take over my life completely, as with some old people I know.

Young Rosemary (right) with Lynne.

I remember a tiny artificial Christmas tree, which had belonged to my late brother, James. There were eight small wax candles tied to the ends of the branches and we lit them on Christmas Day for ten minutes. I can still sense the joy and the glow of the candlelight. Those tiny and very short-lived flames burn in my heart to this day, and with all the happiness there is also the poignant memory of sadness that James was no longer there to enjoy his little tree. We treasured his only surviving possession – the Christmas tree – and remembered him fondly every year.

But my mum and dad did everything they could to make us girls feel loved and special. My stocking, I can remember, was full to bursting: a tangerine, sweeties, nuts, an orange, a tiny gift, and a two-shilling piece, which was called a "florin" in those days. A florin was actually the equivalent of our 10p coin today, but it was worth far more than that – it was the price of five school dinners for a week; it paid for the cinema, ice cream, and a bag of chips for sixpence on the way home!

I had various pets over the years: Billy the tortoise, a one-eyed cat, a green budgerigar. My favourite was a black and white mongrel dog called Bimbo. She was my best friend. She slept with me and my sister in our double bed and I can still recall the lovely feeling as she snuggled under the sheets and curled up beside me. She helped to keep me warm during the terrible cold nights. Winters were freezing in our house without any kind of central heating. We didn't even have a proper hot-water bottle, but Mum improvised, using a large pop bottle filled with warm water, which she

Lynne and Rosemary as they grow older.

wrapped in an old cardie and placed at the bottom of the bed to keep our feet warm. Despite her best attempts, it's not surprising that I suffered from chilblains. Occasionally, my sister and I compensated for the extreme cold by having very heated arguments… usually about whose turn it was to brave the howling gales and empty the potty in the outside toilet.

It's amazing to think of it now, but we didn't have a bathroom then. We had to strip-wash at the sink every night. Friday night was special because it was Bath Night,

Lynne, Rosemary, cousin John and dog Bimbo
on Monk Street.

when we were scrubbed down in a tin bath beside the fire. On Saturday, Mum heated up extra pans of water to top up Friday's bath water, so she could do our weekly wash by hand. She would dry our clothes on the line in the back yard or on a wooden rack hoisted high above the kitchen fire.

I can still hear my dad's clogs echoing on the cobbles after an evening of drinking beer at the local pub. Wooden clogs are a rarity now, but they will always be clopping along, a little unsteadily in my mind, like the soundtrack of an old film – with a lonely figure under the lamplight. And I can hear the floorboards creaking softly as my mum prepared for an early shift at the mill, from 6 a.m. to 2 p.m. Usually, she would be up as early as 5 a.m. She would always look into our bedroom and, one cold morning, I remember that she saw I was awake. She smiled and hurried downstairs. I could hear her frying an egg for breakfast and, moments later, she appeared with a small slice of her egg butty. It was delicious. She had given me most of her egg yolk, the best bit. That simple act made me feel that I was the most important person in her life. She loved me so much that she gave me the best bit.

This is a treasured memory, and it has had a huge impact on my life. I learned that it's good to give the best away, always to give your best.

Rosemary with her parents.

CHAPTER THREE
Courtship and Marriage

I have followed my mother's example of trying to give my best in all circumstances – and this has included decorating homes as beautifully as possible, sometimes with very few resources, and also trying to make myself look as good as possible even when there has been no money at all. Perhaps I am glamorizing the past a little, but I like to think that a little home-made dress of mine had a very far-reaching effect…

I was sixteen years old and up to that time there had been only a few casual boyfriends. This was all about to change as I walked (perhaps not so innocently) up the street. A very cheeky and persistent young man, aged nineteen, fancied me as he saw me walking some way ahead, wearing my own creation, a navy and white spotted dress, and

Rosemary wearing the blue spotted dress that caught John's eye.

John's family: Joe, John, Donald and Hannah.

high-heeled white stiletto shoes with matching roses on the front. He was observing me from behind and, in his own words, he thought: "What a great butt; I can't wait to see the front – wow! She must be a stunner!"

That was the beginning of a campaign. John pursued me for weeks. I was very shy and I ignored him as best I could. But then I relented. Why? It's an old story. He had a very nice car (it was his dad's, actually, but it still gave him the air of a man about town). Before long, I was sitting in the front seat, feeling like a queen as I was chauffeured to the Locarno Ballroom in Blackburn.

Of course, I thought he was a show-off. He wore a grey suit with the latest drainpipe trousers, winkle-picker shoes, and a ghastly turquoise waistcoat that his mum had made.

He had a huge quiff in his hair and – all right, I admit – a lovely smile, displaying a perfect set of teeth. It didn't take long before I was charmed by his winning personality and his ability to make me laugh.

John Lancaster had been a clever and likeable opportunist from an early age. When he was a small boy at Barrow Village School, the headmaster chose him to run the morning biscuit stall. He soon grasped how to profit from this venture, even if it was only by stuffing himself with all the broken biscuits that were left over. He moved from crumbling biscuits to a more enduring kind of investment: collecting stamps. He became a regular schoolboy philatelist, making up his own packets of stamps and selling them at a profit. The young entrepreneur was already on his way…

But even as a little lad he experienced real struggle and humiliation in trying to fulfil his destiny. Although he was a bright boy, clearly expected to pass the 11-plus exam, when faced with the paper and all the pressure of expectations his mind went completely blank. In a nervous panic, he wet himself. As everyone knows, such vivid childhood traumas stay in the mind and heart for a very long time. John had to battle intense feelings of failure and shame at letting down the headmaster and school staff, all of whom had placed high hopes in him for the future, and this was an even worse feeling than the painful embarrassment of his nervous reaction to the exam.

These were the days when to fail the 11-plus would mark you out as a second-rate student, when it could hang like a judgment over your life. If you failed the 11-plus, you couldn't go to grammar school and you would be sent to the local secondary modern school. This could feel like a sentence, rather than an opportunity (as all education should be), and you could find yourself surrounded by low achievers and stuck in a world of low self-esteem. John certainly felt a complete failure at secondary school. He put on lots of weight during puberty and he was regularly bullied. Rough lads would wait for him on his way home from school, drag him down a back street, and beat him up – an ordeal that he never shared with his parents, because he did not want to cause a scene or make things worse.

But, all through these struggles, John somehow maintained a cheerful attitude to life and gladly seized any opportunities for enterprise. He offset his disasters at school by being a butcher's boy, delivering meat from an old black bicycle with a huge basket on the front. He cycled many miles, delivering joints of beef and lamb to homes far and wide, and he was often rewarded with a fabulous meal at the end of the day, cooked by the butcher's wife. Even at the age of seven he worked at weekends and during holidays on milk rounds and helped the local farmer with haymaking. John was an incredibly hard worker, never short of motivation when he was really interested in something – and, in this case, his motivation was increased by the prospect of more wonderful dinners brought to the field by the farmer's wife: bread, cheese, home-made cakes – a country feast worth all the toil and sweat of the morning.

He was a happy-go-lucky lad in so many ways, enjoying fishing with his dad, and the customary delights of a little pocket money – a weekly bar of chocolate from the local post office and a tin of condensed milk, which he would hide under the bed, away from the eager fingers of his brother Donald.

John loved birds – especially yellow, green, and blue ones! – and, even in this childhood passion, he was able to see business opportunities. He used to breed his budgerigars very successfully and would spend hours trying to get them to talk. One day, a customer came to buy one, but just before he arrived the budgerigar started to talk for the first time. John realized that he could get more money from this, so he quickly swapped it for a mute one.

In his final year at school, he decided to work hard. Although he left without any significant qualifications, his determination to do well increased. But his employer refused day release for further education, so John travelled ten miles by bus three nights a week to go to college, eventually gaining his City and Guilds Electrical Installation Certificate.

John's first paid job was as an apprentice at the Dynamo Engineering Company in Clitheroe. He had a very hard time with his boss, who regularly bullied him, thumped him, and made him sweep the factory floor constantly. Experiences like this lay behind the development of a very different approach to industrial relations when, years later, he would run his own business. The welfare of his staff mattered hugely to John, because he knew what it was like to feel literally downtrodden. Again, he said nothing about his sufferings at home. He quietly carried on, without fuss – and would use his growing experience to rewire the houses of family and friends after work. Aged twenty-one, he was able to leave the harsh apprenticeship and take up a job as an auto electrician at the local Vauxhall dealers.

Life began to look up. John was offered the use of a car so he could attend breakdowns and, with his father's help, he soon passed his driving test at the first attempt. The garage was delighted and before long installed a telephone in his parents' house, so that John could be on call. A phone was a very big deal in those days and John's family was the talk of the street. This was a world where hardly anyone had a telephone and it was a huge status symbol… so different from our "global village" of millions of mobile phones and GPS systems. It's really hard to imagine the impact of one single, heavy, old-fashioned phone in a simple terraced street in Clitheroe!

Yes, things were definitely looking up for John Lancaster, a very good-looking young man, with access to cars, an outrageous quiff, and an eye for an attractive girl.

Luckily, that girl turned out to be me.

I must admit that when John presented me with two tickets to the Beatles concert at the Imperial Ballroom in Nelson, I couldn't resist. I screamed throughout the performance. The rather more famous John (Lennon) had my undivided attention for the entire concert.

But the electrical engineer from Clitheroe had made a very shrewd investment with those two tickets. The impact of the concert on me was like wildfire spreading through all my emotions… I didn't need much persuasion to say "Yes" when the young and suave Mr Lancaster finally popped the question.

John sporting his quiff, winkle picker shoes and drainpipe trousers, with Rosemary.

John and Rosemary on their wedding day.

We were married in 1966 at Trinity Methodist Church, Clitheroe. It was certainly a day of overwhelming joy, but also tinged with sadness. My father was so ill in hospital that he was unable to give me away. Our wedding reception was held in the Starkie Arms Hotel. My Uncle George was so drunk when he stood up to make a speech that he kept slurring his words: "Lllaaaaaaddddies…!"

John shouted out, "First door on the right, George." Everyone howled with laughter, except George, who was still trying to finish his sentence.

Following the reception, we visited Dad in hospital. As I walked down the ward towards his bed, I felt like a film star in my empire-line wedding dress – my own creation of sateen, with ribbon lace sleeves and a long train. I will never forget his look of sheer pride as he held me and gave me a long kiss on the lips. I also remember how I sensed, at that moment, his deep sadness at missing his own daughter's wedding. It was so poignant as one of the nurses took a "hospital wedding photo": Mum, my sister Lynne, and her husband Keith on one side of the bed and John and me on the other, with Dad in between, smiling through his pain and squeezing my hand.

With Rosemary's dad in hospital on the wedding day.

We set off later that evening for our honeymoon. Our first night was in Birmingham, which doesn't sound very promising. And it wasn't. We were total innocents, completely inexperienced and unprepared. Unlike today's weddings, which are often more like a tenth anniversary of the first night, this really was our first night. I have to say, despite our fumbling ineptitude, there was something very special about "keeping ourselves" for marriage like that. It's a little sad that this idea has come to be regarded as so old-fashioned. For us, it was the true beginning of marriage and a lifelong bond of the greatest friendship. Typically, we celebrated our new "bond" with helpless laughter early the following morning, when a cleaner burst in by mistake to find herself surrounded by clothes in disarray and two naked people giggling under a sheet. She apologized profusely in her Brummie accent and made a very hurried exit.

So much for empire-line wedding dresses and romantic dreams…

But the first two heady days of our honeymoon in London were incredible. It was my first ever visit to a city, and I was mesmerized by the sights: Buckingham Palace, the Changing of the Guard, the dome of St Paul's Cathedral, the Tower of London, the incredible skyline from the huge River Thames, the glittering nightlife – London! It really was a romantic place to us and we never guessed, two wide-eyed tourists from Clitheroe, that one day this great city would be the scene of an astonishing business breakthrough for John in an event that would change our lives, and the lives of so many, for ever.

We were gloriously innocent and certainly poor then, but truly, richly blessed in love and family. I certainly felt that everything was completely perfect in my life at that point, and that nothing could go wrong. I loved being in love – and being married.

As if things couldn't get better, I was ecstatic when I discovered that I was pregnant the following July, in 1967. However, just as illness had cast a shadow over my wedding, now there was a much more cruel twist of fate. My father died in November. He had desperately wanted the joy of becoming a granddad, but it was not to be.

John and Rosemary in Trafalgar Square during their honeymoon.

The night before he died, I made him some ham and pea soup. I remember taking him the soup, carrying it so carefully and helping him awkwardly to a few mouthfuls. That was all he could manage. "Aye, that's good, lass." Then I talked about the baby clothes and cot sheets I had bought earlier in the day. He smiled faintly. We talked very softly for a while and then he drifted off into a peaceful sleep. He was admitted to hospital in the morning, because his only kidney was barely functioning.

Tragically, he died all alone, because Mum had to go to work and couldn't take another day off to be with him. People couldn't just take time off in those days. There was no such thing as "compassionate leave". You were always in danger of losing your job if you put a foot wrong. If Mum didn't work, she didn't have money, and, of course, Dad understood, because that's how it was.

All alone…

It still makes me feel desolate when I think about it. We all went to the mortuary the next day to identify Dad's body. We were utterly devastated.

The one saving grace was that his life of suffering and pain was over for him, at last, and he was at peace. I noticed that his rosary and cross were in his hand and I recalled Dad telling me, a year before (following yet more painful surgery), that he felt he really couldn't go on any more. He had confided this desperation to the hospital priest on the ward.

"Now, Jim," the priest had said very gently, "take this rosary, hold it close, and remember our Lord; He'll bring you peace." That evening my father slept well and he believed that God had touched him in a special way.

As I look back, I am so sad not to have had more time to share my own Christian faith with him. But all that matters is that my dad met his Maker and found true healing, love, and peace for ever. This knowledge was a huge source of comfort all those years ago – and still is today.

Soon my sadness turned to euphoria when Julie Rose was born on 27 March 1968. My mum was in her element. She used her two weeks of strictly allocated holiday to care for us: cleaning, washing, and making sure mother and baby were looked after with the greatest devotion.

Motherhood was fantastic. I know how people nowadays like to talk of all the stress and strain, the tiredness, the broken nights, the screaming babies… it's almost fashionable to go on about the burdens of motherhood. But honestly, I loved every minute of it.

Our family was complete when, on 3 September 1969, our son, Steven John, was born. It was the same year that Neil Armstrong walked on the moon, but I felt that I had got there before him… I was really riding high on motherhood!

What an adventure it was being a full-time parent: caring, feeding, taking off the towelling nappies that had to be washed in those days, potty training, learning to walk, talk, playgroup, first days at school, wiping away tears, laughing, encouraging, exploring life together…! Being a "stay-at-home wife and mother" is the best job in the world, in my opinion, and a very significant career.

I realize that times are changing, but I know that my love for my two children – and for all my grandchildren – can

Julie and Steven enjoying bathtime.

never change, except to get deeper, and not a minute spent with anyone in my family can ever be wasted.

Perhaps this ordinary, "common-or-garden" love of children and family has been my degree in "the University of Life", my training ground for an extraordinary privilege – a destiny of love and caring for a much bigger family around the world.

But this is to jump ahead in our story, which is only just beginning.

CHAPTER FOUR
Family Life

My earliest memories of the children still bring me so much pleasure. I often think of Julie's adorable smile when she recognized me – she must have been about seven or eight weeks old when she first lit up my life with that smile.

She's been smiling ever since, always ready to laugh, always full of energy. She never kept still even before she could walk; she had her bottom in the air trying to do topsy-turvy roly-polies, which later became acrobatics. Julie

Julie and Steven enjoying their first canoe.

Julie showing off her gymnastic skills at the beach with Steven and dad.

became very good at gymnastics – she had a natural flair at school. It's amazing how character and talents establish themselves so early. Perhaps this is why I have always been so delighted to watch all my grandchildren grow up – parents and grandparents can see potential from the word go.

However, I don't suppose my mum could ever have guessed what would become of my life. Her job was to love me and believe in me, which she always did – and she truly believed in Julie and Steven. They adored her, and one of the highlights of their later childhood was spending a whole year living with their grandma – both Julie and Steven say that it was one of the happiest times of their lives. But more on that later…

It's amazing to think back to that world of the late 1960s,

when Julie and Steven were born. It was the "Swinging Sixties" and a time of great social and political upheaval. The year 1968 was one of student revolutions, the invasion of Czechoslovakia by the Soviet Union, the horrors of the Vietnam War, and the assassination of Martin Luther King, the great civil rights leader who dreamed of freedom and equality for people of every colour, creed, race, and nation. Dr King paid for his inspiration and courage with his life. In many ways it was a disturbing and very unstable world (not so different from the overwhelming troubles in many countries today).

But, by contrast, our little family world in Clitheroe was remarkably simple and secure. It was a time when you could leave your children in their pram, outside a shop or your front door, knowing they would be completely safe. Children played on the streets for hours, without an adult in sight. We didn't live in a world obsessed with "stranger danger" or endless health and safety rules. There was a strong sense of community and families looked out for each other. Of course, we didn't have much, but we had enough food to eat, we had clothes, we had a cosy little house. John worked extremely hard to make this possible, leaving early in the morning and coming home late, and all Saturday too. But I was never lonely, because there were lots of young families on our estate, Edisford Park.

Later in life, I have been privileged to travel widely, but I have often been deeply shocked to see the suffering of many children and families in other parts of the world. My eyes have been opened to how much we really had in those years,

Happy days at Edisford.

even though – by British standards – we were quite poor.

Of course, as any parent anywhere in the world knows, the most precious gifts you can ever have are your own children – and you are truly fortunate if you can look after them well. I am glad that I really celebrated those early years with Julie and Steven.

Memories come flooding back of my passionate love of fresh air and the great outdoors – I would wrap Julie like a little Indian baby in a papoose and lots of blankets and walk for miles, singing songs and talking to her, and I could see her little face under the covers and hear her coocooing. During frosty, snowy weather, her chubby cheeks got chapped and she looked as if she'd fallen into a pot of rouge, with her bright red cheeks.

There are seventeen months between Julie and Steven. The day after Steven was born, John brought my mum and Julie to visit us in Bramley Meade Maternity Home. Unfortunately, children weren't allowed in (only out!), so Mum held her up to the window so I could see her. I can still see her cheerful little face and her tiny hands pressed against the glass. In those days, new mothers had to stay in hospital for seven days and babies were kept in the nursery. You only got to hold them at feeding times, but I had baby Steven with me at the time, so Julie first saw her new brother from a distance. It must have been a puzzling encounter: "Who on earth is that in my mum's arms – and why isn't it me?"

Julie adored her little brother and became a little mummy to him, treating him like her dolly. She would push him around the house in her toy pram. Her caring heart was obvious even then and it came as no surprise when she wanted to train as a nurse.

Both Julie and Steven were really no trouble. They had their ups and downs, like all children, but birthday parties were particularly happy times. We would just have cakes and sandwiches and they would invite all their friends to our house. Their favourite game was pass the parcel. I sang and played my guitar, watching closely to make sure all the children got a present to unwrap. Then there was musical chairs, musical statues, and all the children would go home with a piece of cake. This was long before our more sophisticated (and materialistic) age, when expensive "goody bags" have to be provided.

Things were simple for us. Summer holidays often meant

picnics by Edisford River, when the children played in the water all day. There were always plenty of friends to play with on the new estate, and no one seemed to mind the noise of children shouting and laughing. Even older neighbours welcomed them and gave them sweeties.

Of course, it's easy to idealize one's memories, especially of childhood days, but the sense of love and community all around was very strong. The children joined the usual things, Brownies, Cubs, Guides, and Scouts. I used to love taking part in the local church panto every January. I played Principal Boy for eighteen years and I would get wolf-whistles as I walked on stage in my shorts and knee-length boots. I'm rather proud of that…

But John has an even better memory of pantomimes from his family history. John was born in 1942 and the family home was located at the entrance drive to Brockhall Hospital, which was classed in those days as a mental institution. Some would say that John was lucky to live on the outside… ("Come on now, John, it's time to come back in. We know you've escaped"…) His father was a qualified physical education trainer and State Registered Nurse for the institution, but during the war he was asked to work for the local fire brigade. As it happened, he was also the producer of the hospital pantomime, and he excelled at this. During one dress rehearsal, the air raid sirens went off, with their haunting wail cutting through the night sky. Everything stopped as people in the hospital and nearby houses rushed into shelters, cupboards, basements, and cellars. There was a very loud explosion and a shudder through the ground as a

German plane dropped a bomb less than a mile away.

John's father quickly dashed home, still dressed in his Aladdin costume, complete with make-up. He found John's mother, brother, and baby John, hiding under the stairs – but they began screaming because they thought he was a Japanese invader.

I'm sure this hysterical scene could be worked into a future production of Aladdin somewhere…

Perhaps John's restless energy comes from some of the unusual aspects of his upbringing. Like his father, who taught PE, worked for the fire brigade, and acted in pantomimes all at once, John was incredibly busy and entrepreneurial. His numerous business ventures provided a comfortable lifestyle for us, but only because of his flexibility and resourcefulness. When we went through tough times, he even went to work for Blackburn Council as a dustbin man, collecting refuse. He needed money to clothe and feed his family and pay the mortgage. John wasn't too proud to roll up his sleeves and take any job he could. I loved him dearly for that. His activities included an electrical business, selling Crimplene suits, and purchasing a shop storage unit to import deep-freeze refrigerators (which were a completely new thing at the time!). He was always on the lookout for a good business opportunity. As I've said, John was a genuine opportunist. He once overheard a conversation about the initial success of Rolls washing machines, which were really cheap – but also so badly designed that they shook violently as they were washing and sometimes the drums would come off their mountings and rip through the sides of the aluminium cabinets. Many people had bought these twin tubs that spun clothes and, since the company had gone into liquidation, there was a huge problem in getting them serviced. John found out where to get the spare parts, advertised widely, and was soon inundated with business. He eventually became a threat to Hoover's business in the area – so they decided to make him "Hoover Agent" for the district!

John was so inventive that he couldn't resist improvising, even for a simple prop for a washing line. On one occasion, he took a heavy wooden rail that he had found and cut a "V" shape in it and then pointed to it proudly: "There's your washing line sorted!" Unfortunately, one day when he was away on business, I was looking after Steven and Julie and trying to get this very heavy prop under the washing line on a blustery day. I lost my grip on the prop, which then swung back and fell on my head, knocking me out. I was totally unconscious. Steven and Julie remember this vividly, because they were convinced I was dead. Neighbours rallied round and an ambulance was called. I was in hospital for two days, under observation!

No one has allowed John to forget this, nor the time when we had a Ford Fiesta with a ladder rack on the roof and all our holiday luggage was causing the roof to sag. John said, "I have a solution," disappeared into the garage, and came out with a plank of three-by-two timber, to prop up the roof from inside the car. I'm surprised we got out of those cramped conditions still capable of walking upright. Luckily, as life went on, most of John's inventions proved much more successful.

Rosemary and the children enjoying Yugoslavia.

Proper holidays were a great rarity, because John's freelance life and responsibilities made them difficult to arrange. There is undoubtedly a price tag for being successful in business and sometimes, to be honest, it's the family that pays that price. John was becoming a workaholic and, I must admit, we had our rows and difficulties at times. Marriage can be very challenging, even when a couple love each other.

Yet somehow, in spite of all the pressures, we did manage some memorable family holidays over the years. One of the most vivid memories is of the time that John bought a cheap old caravan for £150. I loved it, even with its musty smells, and I made it look very nice and clean, inside and outside. We filled the only cupboard next to the sink with enough food for a week. Clothes were stored under the built-in seats, which served as a bed for John and me. Steven slept on a hammock-type bed that swung precariously over a bench that Julie slept on. This was a real adventure – and we had never travelled as far as Scotland before. It felt as if we were travelling light years away, like the *Starship Enterprise*, launching into the unknown.

It soon smelled like a spaceship, too, because somewhere south of Glasgow we begin to sniff burning rubber and smoke. John pulled into a lay-by. On closer inspection, he could see through a hole in the mudguard, right into the caravan food cupboard. The ageing springs of the vehicle had failed to support the added weight of the cans of food… and the creaking mudguard was now rubbing along the tyres.

We emptied the cupboard and put the food in the boot of the car. The smell of burning rubber vanished, but this was not the end of our Scottish adventure. When we arrived at the caravan site, in the middle of the night, John got lost and began to drive rather aimlessly round this large field without finding an exit. It was completely deserted – a farmer's field – and definitely not the caravan site. John smiled confidently, always a great optimist.

"Don't worry; I've just taken the wrong exit – we're only a few minutes away." This was the point at which he reversed the caravan into thick mud and got stuck. Steven remembers his father, still smiling, saying, "Don't worry; we'll get the car out in no time," at which he accelerated furiously, spinning the wheels uselessly, and splattering our beautiful white caravan with mud… or was it something else?

John got out of the car and there was an all-too-familiar kind of country smell. "Oh no, we've got stuck in the ****!!"

It was a cow field, but the cows were watching from a considerable distance. Judging from the terrible smell, they had left in rather a nervous hurry. Meanwhile, a few rabbits were watching us in surprise, their eyes shining like stars in the glare of our headlights. John trudged off and before long a farmer was pulling us out of the mire with his tractor.

There were plenty of good things about that Scottish holiday, but somehow the main thing we all remember is… what went so badly wrong. Perhaps it's because we still laugh about it and even enjoy the disaster, in retrospect. Just like the time, years later, when we had an amazing hydrofoil trip to Venice, one of the most beautiful and romantic places in the world. Unfortunately, it was incredibly hot and the canals were stinky, and, for one reason or another, as we walked over the legendary Bridge of Sighs, I fainted in the heat.

Watching his mum collapse onto the stone floor, Steven thought, "Oh no, Mum's dead again." It brought back vivid memories of the Washing Line Incident. Only this time, it was even more dramatic. There was soon the sound of an ambulance siren, approaching down the canal. It was an ambulance boat and, according to Steven, Julie, and John, the scene was rapidly turning into something from a James Bond movie. I was picked up, still unconscious, and surrounded by gesticulating people who were babbling in a language none of the family could understand…

My family think that my talent for amateur dramatics can spill over into real life. I wish I had been conscious and able to enjoy this scene, because I love singing and have even sung operatic pieces in public sometimes. I could have sung a dramatic farewell aria as the ambulance boat sped off into the sunset.

Well, there has been a lot of love, laughter, and fun in our family life, alongside the typical difficulties of married life. But there have also been much more serious dramas and challenges, which have taken us to the edge of despair. Yet these deeper and darker moments have been powerful testing times, which have shaped our characters and changed our lives for ever, as you will see.

School photo of Julie and Steven in 1978.

CHAPTER FIVE

Testing Times

In the 1970s John went into the haulage business. He contacted a local company, Ribble Cement, where he knew the transport manager, and asked if there was any sub-contracting work. As usual, John had spotted another gap in the market, and within weeks he had bought a truck with a pressurized container.

As far as I was concerned, this was just another business venture. The truth is, neither of us realized the massive impact this new "opportunity" would have on our lives. It took us both to the brink of disaster, financially and emotionally.

At the end of this disturbing era, we were both different people because we had discovered that our lives needed to be built on an entirely new foundation.

I'll let John paint the background to our testing experiences in his own words:

My early days with the truck involved very hard work. Self-employed drivers have the financial incentive to keep on and on working – you can't take time off sick or have long weekend breaks or holidays – you just have to keep going. On many days I would leave home at 5 a.m. and set off for Morecambe, because at that time they were building the Heysham Power Station. My clients were delighted that I often managed to do three trips a day. In fact, when work was plentiful, I would sometimes work a fourteen-hour day, which (in those days without tachographs) was risky. But all that mattered to me was making money and supporting my family.

Then a great opportunity opened up. There was an oil boom in the Middle East, and these prosperous countries were desperate to get commodities fast, but there was a problem with shipping via the Suez Canal. It was a golden moment (so I thought) for hauliers to take the goods overland. I sold my tanker and bought an articulated F88 Volvo truck. In no time at all, I had a contract to deliver forty-five-gallon drums of paint, all the way from Bury to Tehran.

I had mixed feelings about such a long trip, because Julie and Steven were so young and it would mean many weeks away. I had a co-driver, however, and I thought everything would be fine. The trip didn't begin very well, because I had my injections only a few days before we were due to leave – which made me ill.

None of this made Rose feel any better about my leaving for such a marathon journey!

Back to my perspective on the story. It's true that John looked really dreadful as we said our farewells. As always, though, he kept smiling – albeit a little weakly! – and was full of typical optimistic chatter. But I couldn't help worrying deep down. Bury to Tehran? It all seemed a rather outrageous plan to me and it hadn't got off to a good start.

He phoned me a couple of days into the journey, from Austria, and he was describing the snow-capped mountains, pretty alpine buildings, and bright blue sky. "Someday I'll bring you all out here for a holiday!" His voice sounded cheery enough, though he did admit that he was still unwell. The idea of a holiday in Austria at some far distant date did not calm my nerves.

John was phoning from a call box – there were no mobile phones in those days, and finding pay phones that worked and could make a continental call was often difficult.

After this, I didn't hear anything for a whole week. It was extremely worrying. I had no idea what was happening, but John's epic journey was becoming more and more complicated and, at times, dangerous, as he can explain:

Approaching the border crossing into Yugoslavia, I started to panic. I couldn't find my passport. I decided to take a big risk by hiding in the sleeper bed in the cab (what a crazy thing to do!). We got through all right (nobody suspected anything), and we drove immediately to the British Embassy in Belgrade. It was embarrassing to arrive there with both of us looking scruffy and in desperate need of a shower, and one of us without his passport. The embassy staff were very helpful, however. They fed us and allowed us to sleep there, but it took all of three days to obtain a new passport. It was so frustrating.

We left to go to Turkey. We knew we were going to have to travel through deep snow and had been told we could easily get snow chains in Istanbul. But there were none to buy. We went through Ankara and the snow started getting deeper and the country more mountainous.

As we drove through villages, children begged for cigarettes at the side of the road and I realized that, if we didn't throw a ciggy out, they would break the bonded seal on the wagon, which would cause huge problems at the next customs point. Meanwhile, the wagon was losing traction as we went into the deep snow.

Suddenly, we came across a forty-foot truck and trailer overturned at the side of the road, which had obviously been abandoned. It had snow chains fitted. Bearing in mind the extremity of our situation, we considered this a piece of good luck, and we parked the lorry so we could take the chains off the vehicle. Just then, a Turkish guy jumped out from behind the lorry, shouting loudly! I thought there was going to be a violent scene, but all he wanted was cigarettes. We kept calm and had started to take the snow chains off when suddenly twenty men appeared, running towards us, wielding forks and shovels.

They had obviously claimed the abandoned vehicle for themselves. Fearing for our lives, we nevertheless managed to humour them with cigarettes and even to entertain them with our little video camera. They loved being filmed and became fascinated by our tools and socket set – so much so that they even helped us to put the snow chains on our vehicle.

But this was not the last of our "international incidents".

We continued up the mountain, which was extremely

steep, for fifteen miles, and after a short while the clutch started slipping. It was a nightmare. We had been told not to stop on Tahir Mountain because of the extreme cold. But we had to stop and get some sleep, and, when we awoke in the morning, my hair had frozen to the side window and the fuel pipes had frozen solid. However, we managed to light a fire under the wagon and unfreeze them – a remedy which could have blown us both over the mountain, but luckily it worked out fine. We then continued very slowly to the next village and, on the side of the road, removed the gearbox and clutch plate. We contacted Volvo, with the help of a local villager. The vehicle was under warranty, but we soon realized that we would still have to travel by bus on an eighteen-hour ride back to Ankara to collect the parts.

It was very primitive in Turkey at that time and, while on this bus, I was looking at a lady in a hijab who had only her brown eyes showing. It reminded me of Rose and I couldn't stop staring. Suddenly, this man seemed as if he was threatening to murder me for looking at his wife, and his comrades joined in. I was extremely scared: my co-driver and I were no match for an enraged group of Turkish nationals. I don't know how we managed it, but we got off the bus before them when it arrived at Ankara and legged it at some speed!

After a day's wait, we endured an eighteen-hour return journey on the bus, still worrying about the safety of our vehicle. Finally, we got there, refitted the gearbox and clutch in very difficult and snowy conditions, and set off for Tehran. We went through customs and unloaded our cargo, but then had to take the truck to another Volvo garage because the clutch plate was slipping again… we needed a completely new pressure plate. It took four days for the truck to be repaired and then more time for the payment to clear, courtesy of the guarantee from Volvo.

Our stay in Tehran was just another terrible experience – with many awkward moments, including when I was asked by another man if he could take me out for a drink, then on to the cinema…

The day came when the truck was ready and I was so frustrated by all the complications that, on leaving the garage, I slammed it into reverse gear too fast – damaging the wing mirror on a passing bus. The driver jumped out and went ballistic at me, but I'd had enough and drove off at speed. To my surprise, he started chasing me, flashing his lights and trying to pass me on a very narrow street in central Tehran. He was so incensed that he overtook me on the wrong side of the road and drove straight across my path, so I had to jam the brakes on. Things were clearly getting very nasty…

You must remember that I knew nothing of all these adventures, only the grim silence of the phone for a whole week. I had plenty to worry about but I was trying to be brave for the sake of the children, and to carry on as if everything were fine. "I'm sure Daddy will ring soon…"

Then the phone rang, but it wasn't Daddy. I heard the *click*, *click* of a continental connection and then a lady spoke in broken English: "I call to tell you, your husband John is in hospital. He is all right." Then the phone went dead.

The words were ringing in my ears, tearing at my heart.

I tried desperately to reconnect with the call, but it was hopeless. I rang John's dad and he said he would contact the British Embassy. They made enquiries in Ankara in Turkey – nothing. I didn't leave the house for six days in case John phoned us.

My mind was playing tricks on me. I feared the worst, and friends came round every day to pray for us and support us. I was living a nightmare, trying to be strong for the children, who kept on and on asking, "When is Daddy going to phone?" I would whisper, "Perhaps tomorrow," when my heart was saying, "Perhaps never."

It was such a strange time, imagining myself a widow at such a young age. My thoughts were in turmoil. I still tucked the children up in bed, keeping to simple routines; I still sang songs to them – but in reality I needed someone to sing songs to *me*.

One evening, I sat down in the lounge and put on the album *Jesus Christ Superstar*. My heart felt so heavy, and I was truly lost and alone. Then, suddenly, I was drawn to a haunting melody, Mary's song:

I don't know how to love him,
What to do, how to move him.
I've been changed, yes really changed...

Mary had known many men, yet having met Jesus she was experiencing feelings that she was finding difficult to process. Jesus had moved her in such a way that His pure love had broken down her defences. She was overcome by

His passion and concern for her. Her encounter with Jesus changed her life. She realized the futility of her past: so many years wasted, seeking love in the arms of strangers, when all she needed was to be loved for who she was. His eyes pierced her soul, His touch moved her heart, His compassion gave her hope, and yet filled her with fear and confusion too.

It was an encounter with the Son of God so powerful and consuming that she was unable to walk away.

My tears flowed. I needed John's loving touch, the warmth of his eyes. My heart was breaking. I felt like Mary, frightened, scared, confused, and lost. I cried out to God, "What's it all about?" Then, suddenly, my heart was filled with an amazing sense of peace. I felt the embrace of the One who is invisible. I knew that, whatever the outcome, even if John were lost to me for ever, all would still be well.

I was at peace.

Later that evening, my neighbour came to see if there was any news. She was amazed at my composure.

"Marie, I have accepted that I may never see John again."

"Never see him again? But…" She gazed at me in astonishment.

"Perhaps never, but I have peace in my heart. I know that we are all in God's hands; He will take care of us, no matter what the outcome."

I slept well that night, for the first time in ages – only to be woken by the phone!

I ran down the stairs and lifted the receiver, my heart pounding as John's voice spoke, loud and clear: "Hi, Rose, how are you all?"

I could hardly speak. My throat was dry. Finally, I blurted out, "Are you better?"

"Better?"

"Which hospital are you in?"

"Hospital?" He was as confused as I was. "I've just had a bit of a set-to with an Iranian bus driver, but no blows were exchanged. The police arrived and we realized we just had to hand some money to everyone, bribery sort of job; anyway…"

I was in floods of tears at the mere sound of his voice and his comical way of putting things. It was crazy, but emotionally it was like experiencing a resurrection!

"So you haven't been hurt…"

"No, no."

"You're completely all right?"

"I'm all right but I'm knackered. And the truck's knackered, pretty much. Bloomin' Turkish mountain roads!"

As John chattered away, and the dream that he was quite all right after all began to become a reality, my eye wandered over to our old black family Bible, which was lying open on the floor. Julie and Steven had been looking at the illustrations of Abraham holding high a knife, ready to sacrifice his son. Immediately, the story came back to me vividly. The voice of God, calling, "Abraham! Abraham!" and the old man looking up, startled: "Here I am, Lord." "Do not lay your hands upon the lad. Now I know that you trust me, because you have not withheld your son, your only son!" There, in the corner of the old engraving in the Bible was a picture of the ram, caught in a thicket… and I remembered the story from church and Sunday school, how God had provided the ram as a sacrifice instead. I knew that this was one of the most important stories in the Bible and I could still hear the haunting notes of Mary's song… "I don't know how to love him…" How could anyone love Jesus enough, since He had rescued us all, by giving Himself as a sacrifice? He is the Lamb of God.

It's amazing how time stretches out, because all this took place in my mind and in my heart in the space of a few moments, but I knew that God was speaking to me – through Mary's song, through John suddenly being given back to me, through the incredible story of Abraham.

Abraham was tested to the extreme, not to cause him to fail but to strengthen his heart and his faith – just as iron ore is purified in the fire to extract precious metal. Sometimes, it is only in the hardest times that we can discover the truth about ourselves and the most precious thing in our lives, which is love – human and divine.

God never intended Isaac to be sacrificed, but He did intend that Abraham would discover that his faith was strong and that God was completely faithful.

Was I being tested too? Had God allowed the strange and challenging circumstances, which had whipped up a storm of fear in me, for some other purpose? Had God chosen John's crazy adventures (any one of which could have ended in tragedy) to lead me to a place of total dependency on Him? Up to this point John had really been the centre of my life, but, although I loved him so deeply, I knew that this priority had to change.

The memory of this profound moment still humbles my heart. From this point, I faced the future knowing, deep down, that my life would never be the same again. I would learn from this gruelling experience not to hold on to things too tightly. I realized that life is a journey full of adventure… and that something quite wonderful had happened. I had truly begun a quest that Jesus Himself described as a search for "the pearl of great price".

Our reunion two weeks later was very special. John was different. He had endured many setbacks on his trip and had passed through a great deal of fear and frustration. I knew that God was at work in both of us, in some mysterious way, but I could only speak for myself. From this day forward, I knew that I was called to be like Mary, sitting at the feet of Jesus and pouring out my love to Him.

Two hundred and fifty years ago, the poet Kit Smart, who struggled so much with his heart and with his troubled mind, wrote these words:

In my nature I quested for beauty but God,
God hath sent me to sea for pearls.

Soon, John had to dive down to an even deeper and darker place to find the pearl of great price. He knew that I had gone through a powerful experience of God and had moved from being a "believer" to being a "follower"… And I don't suppose, at this point, he really understood what all this was about, although he liked what he saw!

The truth is, I had moved from a dutiful, and sometimes rather vague, kind of religion to a very serious commitment.

Some people like to call it "being born again", but I can only describe the change as the difference between having a polite acquaintance with God and a passionate love affair. To know Him in this new way was thrilling, overwhelming, and empowering. My heart was truly on fire.

Meanwhile, John was safe and well and happy to have made it back to "Blighty" (good old England!). He resolved never to drive a truck to Tehran again. But beneath appearances things were not going well. He carried on with his business, which seemed profitable, but it was this haulage business to the Middle East that nearly destroyed him.

I'll let John tell you the story in his own words again, because this was the time when God decided to deal with John as decisively as He had dealt with me:

After my eventful trip to Iran (I didn't make a penny out of that crazy venture!), someone told me that these trips could be really profitable if you dealt with the right company. We were recommended to a London company that had been established in the shipping industry for many years. They said they could offer us lots of trips to the Middle East.

Over the first year we did quite well, renting trucks and employing sub-contractors for journeys to Saudi Arabia. However, we came up against a serious cash-flow problem because we were owed money for quite a number of trips. We decided we needed to visit the company in London. I remember vividly walking into the office to see the managing director behind his big desk. He was a small man, wearing sunglasses. It felt weird, almost like a scene from a gangster movie. The man waved his hand impatiently: "Who are these guys?" He clearly had no idea that we were working for his company. We explained that we hadn't been paid in a long while and he sat there in silence. Then he nodded slowly. "Leave it with me. We'll get it sorted."

I guess in the movies that would have been, "We'll get you sorted". How did a lad from Clitheroe get himself into this? It was all so surreal, and about to get much worse.

Some money did come through to us, but there was still a lot missing. I was just wondering what to do next when I had a phone call. It was a man from the Fraud Squad. He informed me that they were undertaking an investigation of haulage companies that had been working for this London outfit.

The case dragged on for two years, during which our haulage business collapsed. I was involved in another enterprise at this time, a development to build a squash club at the prestigious Belvale Rugby Club. But the fraud investigation cast a shadow over this. Everything in my life was being affected.

We were informed that the hearing would be at the Crown Court in London and that two haulage companies had been found guilty of colluding with the management of the London company in falsifying invoices. Our case was the last to be heard. It was a tough business, getting a barrister and being summoned by the police. I had to go to Blackburn Police Station, have my fingerprints taken, and spend a couple of hours in a cell awaiting my dad, who was on his way to bail me out. It was incredibly worrying for all of us.

I travelled down to London, only to hear from Rose that

proceedings from the first and second day of the hearing were all over the papers. Imagine that… billboards all over Ribble Valley in Lancashire, saying "LOCAL HAULIER IN FRAUD CASE – CROWN COURT IN LONDON!" We were naïve country boys up against the sharp City boys of London.

Belvale Rugby Club rang Rose, deeply worried about their reputation, and we were both very anxious about all the money that was invested in the new squash-club venture.

I knew Rose was praying every day about the court case. This meant a lot, but I still felt very alone, facing what seemed like increasing darkness.

The next morning, I got into the lift to the courtroom and one of the senior managers from the London company was in there with me, handcuffed to a police officer.

"I'm going down," he said grimly – and he wasn't referring to the lift – "and I'm going to take you with me, Lancaster." He was really angry, because our queries about the money owed to us were what had started the whole investigation.

Inside, I was distraught. How could I ever go back to Clitheroe and hold my head up again? I hoped, desperately, that I would not be found guilty.

Back home with the children in Clitheroe, I was praying with all my heart, but I could not conceal my distress. Steven and Julie remember me crying at night. Their daddy was away again, and they were used to that, but something was very different and troubling to them about all this. When they asked me why I was crying, I blurted out, "I don't know if your dad's coming home."

They were always expecting him to walk through the door sooner or later, usually with some presents, so this was a real shock to them.

"Not coming home?" I never mentioned prison to them, but my heart was breaking. Of course, I didn't want to upset them in any way, but I didn't want to hide everything either. We had to hold together as a family, and I would pray with them at night as best I could – choosing my words very carefully.

But our distress was nothing compared to the despair that John was feeling. He had sunk to the lowest point in his life.

I was now in terrible desperation.

The evening before the final day of the court case, I was in my London hotel. But I felt I had fallen to the very bottom of a pit. My world had ended. Even loving thoughts of my beautiful wife and children couldn't help me. For the first time in my life, I really cried out to God: "I have made so many mistakes in my business, but You know my heart; let justice be done. I am innocent of this charge. God help me…!" I was in tears, but I kept on praying. "I know I am guilty of many other things… I have neglected my wife and family; I have been consumed by my work…." This thought, on top of all my other troubles, was tearing me apart. I felt I had hurt my own family so badly. I could only cry out to God, "I'm not interestedin being rich, I only want to provide for those I love, please give me another chance; please forgive me."

Suddenly, to my amazement, I immediately felt so peaceful but so exhausted that I fell into a deep sleep.

How does one explain such experiences? I don't know, but it was one of the greatest and deepest and truest moments of my whole life.

God was there for me.

I awoke in the morning. This was it – I had been given a second chance at getting life right! I had breakfast and I felt totally assured of the day's outcome. To the astonishment of my business partner and my barrister, I even bought our first barbecue set on my way to the courtroom, and put the box under my seat (something which would never be allowed today)! I was so confident that everything was going to be OK and we would soon be celebrating at home.

Sure enough, the judge acquitted us.

And, sure enough, Rose, Julie, Steven, and I celebrated with a barbecue in Clitheroe.

Well, that's the end of a long saga, but it's at the core of my story – and it was the beginning of amazing things to come. I hope that you'll allow me a moment to reflect, because I've travelled a fair distance on my life's journey already, in these early chapters.

I believe that God delights in touching the heart not just of one person, but of two – a marriage; and of four – a family; and of thirteen – grandparents, parents, and grandchildren (my family). He loves to bless whole families through the generations. He loves to bless villages, towns, and nations. He delights to touch anyone, however low they have fallen and however many doubts and questions and problems they have. He is always looking for open hearts, people who are seeking more than their own fortune and welfare, people who are seeking the "pearl of great price". Sometimes, we have to be on the verge of losing everything before we can recognize the treasure that is shining right in front of us.

The kingdom of heaven is like a merchant looking for fine pearls. When he found one of great value, he went away and sold everything he had and bought it.

Matthew 13:45–46 (NIV)

CHAPTER SIX

The Rise of Ultraframe

Somebody once said, "To be afraid of risk is to be afraid of life." John was very courageous when it came to taking calculated risks in business. He always weighed everything up carefully, researched the market, and asked for second opinions. He was never too proud to seek advice. But he also knew his own mind and was ready to step out and have a go when others would have played safe, settling for security and safety. The truth is that a great many people settle for less when it comes to their career, their finances, even their relationships and their vision for life.

But John, a lad who had left school without qualifications, always had big ideas – and, much more important, was prepared to take some amazing risks. He was ready to pay the price for his ambitious schemes, in time, money, and lifestyle. Being married to John has often been scary, but it has never been dull!

Our life, as you have seen so far, has been a real roller coaster. However, although a roller coaster has many ups and downs, the main idea is to have fun. And we have had a great deal of fun and fulfilment, especially since 1983 when John started his most successful enterprise, Ultraframe, which was to change our lives for ever – and the lives of many others too.

The first brave decision we had to make, around this time, was to sell our house in Fairfield Drive. We needed the money to raise some capital for business, although John had also spotted a barn with an acre of land, which he thought he could renovate himself in his spare time. Spare time! John has always had a great sense of humour, and this was certainly one of his best jokes.

Well, first of all, John and I landed up living with friends for nearly a year, while Julie and Steven lived with my mum down the road. Then, as the timescale for the barn conversion expanded (indefinitely), John bought a caravan, which he installed on the site. As it turned out, this became our home for five years.

Steven remembers the *Star Wars* wallpaper in his bedroom – "if that's what you could call it" – and the endless condensation on the windows and the walls. "Han Solo looked like he had a snotty nose, with dewdrops running down from it."

Steven and Julie missed Fairfield Drive, where had had plenty of friends to play with on the street, and they missed their amazing time with Lily. My mum was so generous – and they both have wonderful memories of those precious months with her. She she a rented a one-bedroom council bungalow, and she gave up her own bed so that her two grandchildren could share it, while she slept on a couch in the living room (still keeping to her principle of giving the best away). She was so full of love for them, and, of course, she spoiled them and devoted herself to their every whim: the ideal granny! Steven describes her as "an absolute diamond – the person who held everything together for us".

Julie and Steven with their Gran Lil.

I am very proud of Lily's example and hope I can be like her, for the sake of all my grandchildren. Grandparents have a very special role to play when it comes to the stability of families as they go through many challenges in life.

The challenge, at this point, was to accept some of the sacrifices that go with launching a major enterprise. We managed to make the caravan an amazing home, in many ways, and Julie remembers that we had not only a rabbit and a dog in that small space, but a piano! Live music is one of the most precious gifts you can have in any home, and is certainly more important than grand surroundings. Julie also remembers John installing a wood-burning stove and melting the polystyrene tiles on the ceiling. Fortunately, her father's inventions were about to become far more successful than that.

John's breakthrough came when, as an avid reader of *The Sunday Times*, he noticed an editorial about a new product that would revolutionize the building industry: UPVC window frames and doors that would last a lifetime and never need painting. He researched the product and became so enthusiastic that he decided he would start a small cottage industry from the garage, an old Nissen hut beside the barn. He asked a number of friends what they thought about this venture and I remember one close friend saying, "Plastic windows? No… they'll never catch on."

It's always worth remembering how many negative responses you have to face in life, even to great ideas. There were record labels that turned down the Beatles and publishers who rejected the manuscript of "Harry Potter"… and there were probably thousands of people in the Stone Age who thought the wheel would never catch on.

John has always been very persistent, so, even when the council refused him planning permission to convert the garage to a business – on the grounds of "disruption to the peace of the local community"! – he didn't give up. He leased a small industrial building on Waterloo Road in Clitheroe and employed three people, training them to measure, cut, and assemble window frames.

This was certainly a significant risk for us and I had to trust John completely, which I did. The truth is, taking this step of faith financially meant that we would not be able to make the barn into a liveable home and so we would have to spend a number of years living in the caravan.

Together, with Julie and Steven, we happily agreed to this position. Prayerfully we committed, with the support of our church, to asking for God's blessing on this business. John, now forty years old, realized that this might be his final chance to launch a successful business venture. With his amazing self-belief and his new-found faith, he was confident that his moment had finally come…

The manufacturing unit was extremely small, only sixteen hundred square feet, and the machinery was so noisy that we had to stop the large cutter to take telephone sales enquiries. There was no separate office, only a desk in a corner. My job was to clean up, sweep away the ever-growing piles of plastic shavings, brew tea, answer the phone, and, most important of all, encourage the staff. Our first employee called me "Aunty Rose", and this title stayed with me throughout the whole company history.

John worked so hard in those days, starting at 7.30 in the morning and often not finishing till 10.00 at night or later. He was working on improving designs and manufacture, organizing installers, and often visiting customers and measuring up in the evenings. I remember a time when he was in the town centre of Blackburn and was so exhausted that he simply couldn't remember which way to go to return home to Clitheroe. His obsessive hard work certainly gave me cause for great concern at such times.

However, we were soon expanding into the next unit, eventually renting all five on the industrial estate. Demand was growing as Ultraframe's reputation increased. John kept up the pressure on himself and on the business. He loved what he was doing and he found that employing local people was a source of great satisfaction. He had an eye for detail and, when it came to customer satisfaction, he was always thinking ahead. He equipped his fitters with dustsheets and Henry™ vacuum cleaners, and they had to clean every trace of dirt from a job before they left. The customers loved it – good move!

We were soon moving to much larger premises in Kendal Street and employing over fifty people. This was a time when property prices were rising, and many people could not afford to move if they wanted a bigger house. The conservatory demand was in its infancy. However, national planning regulations changed, allowing conservatories to be added without planning permission, saving on time and cost, which catapulted the boom. The models on the market had major roofing problems with leakage and structural stability. John noticed this and decided to design a completely new kind of roof. He even took bits of UPVC to bed with him to play with – although I'm not sure I should admit that my husband was occasionally more interested in lumps of plastic than me.

John was always the eternal child, terribly excited about his new toy. He couldn't sleep for working out angles and gutters! His research and development team were amazed at John's inspiration and the number of ideas churning out of his mind. Eventually, he developed the first of many winning designs that looked good and were easy to install. (It's not surprising that, by the time he retired, the company had registered over two hundred patents.)

John and I had always said that if we were ever successful, we should use our resources to help people less fortunate than ourselves. We continued to pray over the business – a habit which might seem eccentric to many entrepreneurs in the cut-throat business world of today, where love and prayer probably seem like fatal signs of weakness. But we knew that this was God's calling on our lives and we should give Him the glory and look to Him for inspiration. We had close friends who prayed with us and helped us to stay strong and steer clear of many potential pitfalls.

The first big test of our integrity came soon enough. John was offered a huge contract by a manager of a government-run organization. This was a real opportunity to increase Ultraframe's reputation. There would be lots of work ahead and plenty of security – but then, a bombshell! The manager had a little "proviso": "Well... my house needs new windows and doors," he intimated! John knew it was going to take a back-hander to get the contract. At first, John thought this was all right and even gave me reasons why we should agree, but he couldn't persuade me. I felt really strongly that we should not compromise our principles, and eventually John agreed. He could see, as his initial enthusiasm began to come into perspective, that this would be a serious wrong turning. Sometimes we have to recognize such things together, with our marriage partner or our closest friends. It's easy to get carried away with the idea of a "great business opportunity", and many reputations lie in ruins because of this kind of mistake. The decision was truly hard for us, because we were saying goodbye to so much work and potential good publicity, but, as is often the case, once the decision was made we both had complete peace. We knew it was right.

Tests came in every shape and form. I will never forget a late-night telephone call to say that our business premises were on fire! John leapt in the car and the three-minute drive seemed like an eternity. When he got there, without thinking of the consequences and ignoring a fire officer, he rushed into his blazing offices. He was determined to rescue the lifeline of the business, the order book! He made a quick exit with the book and other files, and before too long the blaze was under control.

It had been a major fire, however, and we did not know what we would see when we returned the following morning. I was fearing the worst, but to everyone's surprise, a large number of the display windows had survived the fire intact. John smiled to himself. "Flippin' 'eck! Looks like they're indestructible!" Always the opportunist and clever marketer, John decided to turn disaster into triumph. A few days later, there was a torchlight procession through the town, an annual event, and John had already booked a float to advertise the business. Now he proudly displayed his fire-proof windows. The newspaper headlines were great: "Company takes part in torchlight procession only days after windows survive the test of fire!"

John was soon visiting the site of Atkinson Machinery

in Kendal Street, which was offering some of its industrial buildings for sale. He struck a shrewd bargain and, before long, Ultraframe was in a fifteen thousand square feet factory, that quickly grew to over quarter of a million square feet, with air conditioned offices. This was a great rarity in those days, but it added to the quality of the work environment and the morale of everyone concerned. Meanwhile, John kept his office open-plan – accessible to all on the factory floor – an arrangement which had a very positive impact on communication in a rapidly expanding company. Ultraframe soon had over 100 staff.

Of course, in many ways these were bitter-sweet years because John was so completely absorbed in his business, but he tried hard to show care for his family and our own environment. We were young enough and still happy to be building our dream home, except that for a long time it was far more of a dream than a home... Although the business was developing very well, there was still little money to spare and John would occasionally try to do significant work on the barn himself. At one point, he stripped the stone roof, nearly killing himself when it collapsed under him. It was like one of those silent films with Buster Keaton, or a Bugs Bunny cartoon where Elmer Fudd runs out of a collapsing building covered in dust. John staggered into the caravan covered in mud and bleeding, and said, as if it were the most normal occurrence in his day, "I've just fallen through the roof."

I looked at him and replied in the same matter-of-fact voice, "Oh yes, we heard a bang." There were always bangs and crashes going on as he carried out his demolition work.

All he needed from the doctor was a precautionary tetanus jab. John walked into the surgery holding his shoulder, and walked out holding his bottom.

Another crazy scene from the Caravan Era of our lives was the Clandestine Emptying of the Chemical Loo. This had to be done weekly, and John would sneak out in the middle of the night with a full bucket, across the road and round the corner, to empty the waste into the soil drain outside my mum's council bungalow. On more than one occasion there was an unfortunate mishap, but the main drama came when Mum's toilet became completely blocked. The council workman came, raised the manhole cover, and said, "Eh, missus, tha's been using a reet load of toilet paper. It's like a bloomin' swamp in 'ere." Of course, Mum kept "mum" about John's midnight escapades.

Memories of her love and wonderful good humour, always caring for us, always doing anything for the family, come flooding back to me as I write. But there is one memory that I still find incredibly hard to bear.

It was 1985 and one of the worst days of my life. Mum was taken into hospital with severe abdominal pain. Emergency surgery relieved an abscess in her abdomen, but, with severe peritonitis raging through her body, she never recovered from the surgery. She was soon fading fast.

The drama of that terrible day intensified when Steven was brought into A&E following a road accident – and, for a moment, I thought I was going to lose my mother and my son on the same day. His injuries were not very serious, however, and thankfully he was discharged, recovering over the next few weeks. But there was no hope for my beloved mum.

A young nurse on the ward took me to one side and said, "God is in communication with your mum's spirit now, so encourage your family to pray together and stay calm." Her words had a deep effect on me and, from a feeling of utter helplessness, I began to feel that my life was safe and in control. And, far more importantly, my mum was truly in God's hands. What safer place can there be for anyone, on earth or in heaven? Mum struggled on for four days and then slipped away as Lynne and I held her close. As she was passing, I looked into her face and asked, "Mum, what's it like?" and a peaceful smile spread across her face. She squeezed Lynne's hand and was gone.

All was well, at last…

It's still so hard to write about this. All I can say is, "We all miss you so much, Gran Lil."

She was the salt of the earth. Gentle, hard-working, never complaining even though, throughout her life, she faced one hardship after another. She was constantly saying, "Stop tha' mathering about me; I'm ow reet," in her strong Lancashire twang.

She always thought of others before herself and I still treasure that memory of her smiling and sharing the best bit of her egg yolk with me when I was a little girl. She loved me so much that she gave me the "best bit". This little gesture has had a huge impact on my life, helping me always to give the best away. She took such great delight in her four grandchildren, Julie, Steven, Dale, and Michael.

She said that she had all the happiness she wanted in her "grandchilder, fags, and a beer". What more did she need?

Gran Lil loved simple pleasures, was always content, and was determined not to be a bother to anyone. She never wanted to be a burden to any of us. She was adamant that we had to get on with our lives because she had had her time. Our responsibility was now to our own families and our happiness. Mum knew how to survive as she walked the long road of suffering many times throughout her life, coping as best she could. I still miss her terribly but I am certain of this: she is safe in God's arms and she has left a great legacy of love.

She never lived to see our dramatic success with the soaring business of Ultraframe. But even though so many things were uncertain and half-finished in our lives, she believed in us completely. She might be surprised at everything that has happened since, but I think she would take it all in her stride. She wouldn't make a fuss. She would smile and just be glad that we are "ow reet".

It's true that as we lose important people in our lives, sometimes we gain new friends who become very precious to us. In the years that followed, there were friends who became so close that they were like additions to our family. One very special couple arrived on our doorstep just around the time that our lovely new home was being completed. (I should say that this final miracle of renovation was not John's work but the result of dedicated builders – although John can certainly claim the vision for the project – and Julie,

Steven, and I can claim the patient endurance necessary to achieve it…)

This remarkable couple, who walked into our lives in the 1980s, were Ray and Nancy Goudie, members of a successful band called Heartbeat. They were performing locally and appearing in an arts event for the churches. We had answered a call to accommodate some of the "artistes", and along came this very attractive, very cool, funny, and wacky couple… who brought music, love, laughter, and passionate commitment to arts and faith into our household.

Ray and Nancy were the very first people to stay in our lovely new home, even before we did (I was remembering Gran Lil's principle of the Egg Yolk) – so they were delighted. Steven remembers the many hours that Ray, who was a very good drummer, spent with him, teaching him new skills and encouraging his musical gifts. Both Ray and Nancy touched us so much with their generosity of character, their kindness, their humour, and their insights into faith and life. Great things came from this friendship, but there's a whole chapter dedicated to the story of Ray and Nancy and New Generation Music and, once again, I'm jumping ahead!

Strong, loving, and trusting relationships have always been important to us and, looking back at the amazing rise of Ultraframe in the 1980s and 1990s, I can see that high-quality business practices, clear moral standards, and a vision of caring for the workforce were really at the heart of everything. Just as John and I were being blessed by friendships old and new, by our church, by our family, and by inspirational people who came into our lives, we were being called to lead our amazing workforce by example. We were tasked with modelling a different kind of business success, which was all about sharing and all about people.

I'm so glad that we had our feet on the ground, and that we had been through so much in our lives. I'm grateful for the struggles, and even for the disappointments and the hurtful losses too. I'm thankful that faith in a loving God kept us humble and very dependent, because we were about to experience the kind of success and fortune that is a fantasy for most people – a success which can sometimes destroy families if they let the money, popularity, and illusion of power go to their heads.

But before this incredible good fortune could safely come our way, we had an important lesson to learn. God was calling us to identify closely with the sufferings of others thousands of miles away from our little world in Clitheroe. He wanted us to walk, however fearfully at first, in their footsteps. I can scarcely believe it, looking back, but we were soon to have an astonishing and crazy adventure in communist Russia that I can only regard as a divine dress rehearsal for our many later adventures around the world.

CHAPTER SEVEN
Smugglers

One of my favourite films is *Dr Zhivago*. I saw it at The Grand in Clitheroe in 1966 and I was gripped from beginning to end. For three hours, my life in Lancashire and the whole world of Britain faded away as I found myself overwhelmed by the vast landscape of Russia, from St Petersburg in the west to outer Siberia and the Chinese border, a region covering eleven time zones. I was caught up in the tragedy and the brutal drama of the Russian Revolution, epic landscapes of ice-bound wilderness and dark forests, the imperial grandeur of Moscow, and the poverty of the common people. I was swept along by a passionate story of love, betrayal and doomed romance.

The images from this film, one of the greatest British movies ever made, still haunt me and millions of people who saw this drama in the context of the wealth and self-obsession of the 1960s. It was as if the world of high fashion, pop music, flower power, and free love was suddenly challenged by another, much darker reality. For the Soviet Union, throughout my own lifetime, had become one of the most dangerous places in the world to live… especially if you were a Christian.

The Russian Revolution took place in 1917 and was a time when the old ruling order was brutally overthrown. The Russian Tsar, Nicholas II, and all his family were executed by firing squad. No mercy was shown to anyone who opposed the Bolsheviks, the revolutionary guards under the command of Lenin. Lenin established the world's first communist state, inspired by the theories of Karl Marx, and it is easy to forget the power and the seductive idealism of a vision in which everyone would be equal, land and property would be owned by the state, and the fruits of labour would be shared by everyone.

But Karl Marx, who never lived to see a real communist state, famously wrote that "religion is the opium of the people". He believed that once there was true justice, shared wealth, and equal opportunity, the common people would not need the "drug" of religion to ease their pain. As far as Marx was concerned, religion was finished…

Vladimir Lenin, the leader of the Russian Revolution, took these ideas to heart. He thought that the Christian religion would die naturally, and when it didn't, he and other Russian leaders decided to help it on its way. Russia established the world's first officially "atheist" state. It became increasingly difficult to express Christian belief, especially to talk about faith with anyone else. Sharing the gospel, or "evangelism", became a serious crime. Over the course of the twentieth century, from Lenin to Stalin to Khrushchev to Brezhnev, millions of Christians were persecuted. Huge numbers vanished into labour camps in Siberia; countless people were martyred. Children were taken from their parents and forcibly "re-educated" into atheism.

The seventy years of the Soviet Union were among the darkest in human history and, at the same time, there was terrible persecution of Christians in communist China and in many other regions of the world. The last surviving communist regime today, North Korea, is now the most dangerous country in the world to be a Christian.

When I watched *Dr Zhivago* I was deeply moved, and I was powerfully drawn to Russia and its suffering people, but I had no idea then what it meant to be a Christian under communism. I was young, I had not yet found my own faith, and I suppose I thought that everyone could believe whatever they wished – just like in Britain. But, gradually, the terrible truth was leaking out into the West; writers such as Boris Pasternak, who wrote *Dr Zhivago*, opened the eyes of many to the brutality of the Soviet Union, but Alexander Solzhenitsyn wrote many books that shocked the world. He was a Christian himself and had survived a labour camp. His books were published in the 1960s and 1970s. Meanwhile, stories of persecution and suffering were stirring the conscience of Christian churches that enjoyed so much freedom. Pastor Richard Wurmbrand wrote a famous book called *Tortured for Christ*. He spent fourteen years in solitary confinement in a Romanian jail – imprisoned for his faith. Amazingly, he experienced the presence of God so profoundly that sometimes he would dance and sing praises in his tiny cell. A friend of mine heard Wurmbrand speak in an English church in the late 1960s. The pastor astonished his Western audience by saying that, when he was released from jail, he "came down from the mountain top". He also said, "You people in the West pray for us behind 'the Iron Curtain', but we pray for you behind 'the Silk Curtain'." He could see that people in Britain were imprisoned by materialism and the pursuit of selfish pleasure, and he thought that the Christian church in Britain had become weak because of this.

It's a well-known fact that for a long period, from the 1950s to the 1980s, there was indeed an "Iron Curtain" between East Berlin (part of the Soviet Union) and West Berlin – a wall of concrete, steel, and barbed wire – and the phrase "Iron Curtain" came to signify the huge and deadly division between the free world and the communist world. But Pastor Wurmbrand's words remind us, even today, that it is possible to be imprisoned in more ways than one.

Well, all this is a long background story to the amazing adventure that John and I had behind the Iron Curtain in 1986…

We went to our church one Sunday and there were some guest speakers from Open Doors, the organization founded by the Dutch Christian Brother Andrew. Brother Andrew had become famous for his exploits in smuggling Bibles into communist countries and had written a book with the provocative title *God's Smuggler*.

John and I sat open-mouthed, utterly amazed by their stories of daring trips to secretly deliver Bibles to Russian Christians. Here were people desperate for God's word, hungry for every sentence of Scripture, forced to meet in secret and frequently facing imprisonment and even death.

It was a staggering contrast with our world, where old Bibles lie on bookshelves gathering dust, or are chucked into boxes in our attics, or consigned to a corner of a charity shop… Bibles forgotten, unread, although we have the freedom to read, to learn, to change… to be blessed. It's incredible how we have taken our amazing freedoms for granted! What if we suddenly lost them? Would people in Britain suddenly wake up and realize what glories they have missed?

This story of mine is set in the 1980s, but, even as I am writing, thousands of people are dying in Syria and Iraq simply because they are Christians. To own a Bible, in some places in the world, is still a death sentence.

John and I listened, more and more impressed and troubled by the stories told by our visitors from Open Doors. We heard how Christians were deported to camps in the cold, desolate wilderness of the remote northern Siberian land, the size of an ocean. But, despite the dangers and the suffering, Christians in Russia were desperate for Bibles…

The speakers smiled gently at us and then astonished us. "Would anyone like to join us for a three-week trip to Russia?"

There was silence in the church. It was a very powerful challenge. John and I looked at each other. I knew what he was thinking and he knew what I was thinking.

But John had so much work to do, surely… and this was no time for holidays or even for crazy adventures…

No time… no time for God?

One of the words used in the Bible for time is *kairos*.

And it is much more significant than just time, the passing of days and years; it means "God's time", the "right time" to do something. Looking back, I can see that this moment in our church was a *kairos* moment, because God was calling us to stretch ourselves, take a huge risk, to just follow Him without questioning... and in the future He would ask us to do this more and more.

"OK, then," said John to the visiting speakers. "When can we go?"

"Very soon," came the quiet reply.

Our journey began only a few weeks later.

On our arrival at Open Doors in the Netherlands we collected a caravan, which was to be our home for the next three weeks. We were to be joined by another couple but there was only one double bed to sleep the four of us. I looked at the bed, and thought, "This gives a new definition to the phrase 'close Christian fellowship'." But I wasn't about to complain because I knew there were much more serious challenges ahead.

During our briefing session over dinner, we were informed that the Russian authorities would search our vehicle rigorously and ask many questions relating to our trip. It was illegal for anyone to enter the country in possession of drugs, pornographic literature, or Bibles. I had to smile at this curious list of threats. Perhaps more young people in Britain would read the Bible today if they realized how dangerous and subversive it can be for a society... But I didn't smile at the next comment.

During dinner, our hosts told us they were concerned for two people. They hadn't heard from them for quite some time after they had crossed the border into Russia. They asked us to scan the border compound as we crossed, to see if their vehicle had been impounded. At this point my mind was in turmoil. "What if we get caught? Will we be tortured? I'm scared! Will we see Julie and Steve again? Will we be imprisoned? What are we doing here? I want to go home!"

Needless to say, I didn't sleep a wink that night. But John kept a cool head. He held me and prayed that all would be well. We needed to trust God and believe that He was with us.

Trust God! The simplest words, and yet sometimes the hardest thing in the world to do. I remembered the old hymn chorus:

Trust and obey,
For there's no other way
To be happy in Jesus,
But to trust and obey.

I think it's probably easier to trust when you're five than when you're forty-five. But John and I had passed through many tests before and this one was taking us to a deeper level of trust.

The following morning the two men were asked to meet in the workshop to help load the Bibles into a secret compartment. They were told not to disclose details to the ladies, not wanting to compromise our safety should there be any form of interrogation. John was animated on his return.

"Rose, it's like James Bond's secret service in there; you even have to use a password to get into the place!"

I was not amused, muttering, "What is it, then?"

To which he replied, "Flying Goose." I have to admit that my enthusiasm was at an all-time low. I sighed heavily.

"I don't think I can do this, John."

But soon we were on our way to catch the ferry. I silently prayed, "God, if You are with us, please give me a sign." Soon afterwards, as we drove past a small harbour, I noticed a beautiful wooden sailing ship, which was such a lovely sight. I was astonished to see that she was called "The Flying Goose".

I closed my eyes and whispered, "Thank You, God."

I was much more settled as we embarked the ferry. The spectacular fjords were like a soothing balm to my troubled spirit and my sense of adventure was beginning to surface once more. Our journey took us through Norway, then across Finland – a long drive, in which we all took turns behind the wheel. I was nervous during my first two-hour stint, a double first for me on continental roads and towing a caravan! I was talking silently to myself: "Slowly does it. Let's go a little faster; OK, much faster; yes, I can do this!" My confidence was growing, but suddenly the caravan began to sway from side to side. There was panic in the car! I brought things under control in the nick of time. It was just another "learning curve" – literally. Eventually I got the hang of it, thank goodness. With a few miles still to go, I was resting in the back of the car when something amazing happened. A most glorious sound filled the air. Voices and musical instruments united in a harmonious chorus.

"What is this beautiful music?" I asked our companion, thinking that he was playing a cassette. He replied, "What music? I can't hear anything."

I know it sounds incredible, but this was a very powerful experience.

And suddenly there was with the angel a multitude of
the heavenly host praising God, and saying "Glory to
God in the highest, and on earth peace."

Luke 2:13–14 (ESV)

We were on our journey, and we were not alone…

Prior to crossing the border from Finland to Russia, we found a suitable place to bury our own bibles, cassettes of music and talks, information and briefing instructions, which we all had to memorize. Anything relating to Christianity was forbidden. After a change of clothing, everyone looking neat and tidy, we held hands and prayed together – I was thankful that God had listened to my troubled cry and given me the best reassurance that any loving daddy can give to his precious child: "Do not fear, I am here for you, I love you." Approaching St Petersburg and the border crossing, my first impression was of a prison camp – with high wooden lookout towers, armed guards, and German Shepherd dogs barking fiercely. It was a frightening introduction to a hostile world. We were ordered by a guard to get out of our vehicle. Of course, we all felt nervous and intimidated. Our travelling companion was told to drive the caravan over an inspection pit and he fumbled somewhat, hitting the kerb, almost causing the caravan to overturn. The guards made a thorough search. We heard them tapping, slamming cupboards. They searched high and low. Their faces were cold and menacing. I needed a break from the tension, so I went to the "Ladies" with my female colleague – about the bleakest experience possible. We entered a cold, grey, and stained concrete block, with water dripping down the walls. It was more like a military pill box from the war, an abandoned lookout post, than a reasonable public convenience for tourists! There were no concessions to comfort here. I imagined secret cameras hidden, our conversation being monitored, even though we were chatting about nothing. "So… you are glad you have found your lip salve, Mrs Lancaster! And what secret documents are hidden in this bourgeois Western luxury of yours?" My mind was running riot as always.

Back with the men, we were interrogated for real.

"Why are you here?!"

"Where are you going?!"

"What are your plans for your journey?!"

"Where will you stay tomorrow?!"

I nervously overplayed my passion for ballet, hoping to make a good impression, but it was to no avail. Arts and culture were not high on the list of enthusiasms for these brutal-looking guards. I was soon imagining *Swan Lake* interrupted by a burst of machine-gun fire. However, I did manage to elicit a wry smile when I said "*Do svidanya*" and

"*Spasibo*" – "goodbye" and "thank you". I don't suppose they'd heard Russian spoken with a Lancastrian accent before. Our brief had been to show respect by our appearance and attitude, appear to be tourists, spread holiday brochures across the seats, and leave the Kirov Ballet brochure in a prominent position. Well, perhaps even these rough guards were secretly proud of the great Russian ballet after all…

Following a thorough search of our vehicle and silent prayers from the four of us and many people back home, we eventually got the all-clear to drive through "no man's land", a distance of two miles, to the border crossing into St Petersburg, a truly beautiful city, described as the Venice of the North.

We arrived at our campsite, only to be promptly met by two people whom we suspected were KGB. At that time one in five were agents in the Russian secret service; we were travelling through a world of suspicion. The paradox of the beauty of Russia and its culture dominated by fear and mistrust was vividly portrayed to me by a lovely little hut decorated in Russian art, which stood opposite our caravan. A guard was in the doorway, holding a Kalashnikov, watching our every move.

We told the agents that we were going to visit the Hermitage, one of the most famous art galleries in the world, see the famous sites, attend the Kirov Ballet. They smiled politely and nodded. Did they believe us? Their faces were inscrutable. Everything we said was true, but, of course, there was so much more to our journey. What if we were caught now? Adrenalin began to pump into my stomach and my heart was already beating very fast. I had a lot to learn about being a calm and collected smuggler. Part of me was like a child, on the edge of screaming out, "All right, all right, I confess, it was me; I did it!" I only have to be looked at severely by someone to think I'm guilty. It must go back to my school days…

Meanwhile, John was clearly enjoying all this subterfuge. He was smiling and joking, so relaxed. I reckoned he could apply to be James Bond's apprentice from Clitheroe: "006 and a half". The following day we queued for a bus to take us into St Petersburg city centre. As we were waiting for it to arrive, I noticed a serious-looking lady staring at me. Well, everyone was "serious" – I thought that Russian people in general had a grey pallor and appeared rather sad and sombre. I don't recall one single smile from the people going about their everyday business: communism seemed to crush the joy from their hearts. But this lady was looking at us with a greater intensity than I had seen before. Eventually she approached and, speaking perfect English, asked where we were going. Then she had the effrontery to tell us she would go with us and be our guide. Not wanting any trouble, we agreed, although we all thought she was far too pushy. She was a large lady and this was the era when a Russian shot-put thrower called Irina Press had become famous at the Olympics. I wondered if this lady was a cousin – clearly not someone to argue with!

She said brusquely, "I will take you to underground train."

We walked obediently towards the escalator, but, as I

stepped forward to get on, a huge metal barrier shot straight across my lower leg. The pain in my shins was excruciating. I had tears in my eyes.

John then said, "Uh-oh, we're in trouble."

Towering over us was a thickset female guard, looking grim and powerful in her uniform. Clearly another relative of Irina Press.

"Where is ticket?" she bellowed in English. "Ticket!"

Another mistake… although we were certainly giving an excellent impression of being innocent and stupid English tourists. She took our money and gave us our tickets and opened the barrier. I limped onto the escalator, only to hobble straight into our friend from the bus stop. She looked at me with a kind of harsh satisfaction, as if to say, "Don't think you can shake me off."

But how could we get rid of her? I had a plan. The station was crowded and we jostled towards the platform, our guide leading us very closely, constantly waving us on. The train arrived and the crowd surged towards the doors. We climbed onto the train but, just as the doors were about to close, we jumped off, waving goodbye to a very annoyed lady on the train.

I will never forget the look of anger and dismay on her face.

Was she a secret agent? Or just a woman intent on making money from us? I didn't care, for now I really felt as if I was in a spy film, and I loved it. After all, I was the heroine! We did have a lovely day looking at the sites, like perfectly innocent tourists – and I kept the impression up by starting to cross the road before the traffic control policeman blew his whistle. He went crazy at me, swearing in Russian.

"Good job we haven't got an interpreter," said John.

We also did some shopping that day but I was struck by how dull and bleak so many shops were. There were lots of empty shelves and long queues into the streets, especially for simple staple foods such as bread and vegetables. Even without considering the oppression of a police state, or the persecution of so many Christians, we could feel the weight of sadness and the quiet despair everywhere we turned.

I can only describe the experience as a feeling of darkness, a looming cloud over a whole nation of proud and noble people; so many broken, so many struggling to survive. So many in bondage to fear.

Back at the campsite, we had a heavy downpour one evening, pounding on the caravan roof. With four adults sharing a double bed, you can well imagine that this drum solo, which lasted for several hours, was not conducive to a good night's sleep. But John kept us amused with various comments: "I always wanted to experience the Edinburgh Military Tattoo, but not on top of my caravan in the middle of Russia"… and there were plenty of laughs despite our sleep deprivation.

The following morning, a tall Norwegian man knocked on our door. He was from a neighbouring caravan.

"Have you a problem with your roof leaking?"

We looked but couldn't see any sign of water dripping through.

"There are many holes in my roof; the rain has poured

through. Come and see!"

After this, we inspected our roof and sure enough we had holes everywhere – in the roof and in the walls. What was going on? Then we remembered the strange noises as the border guards had checked out our caravan. One of them had had a metal object strapped to his arm, half-hidden under his sleeve – it was a narrow rod, the size of a pencil.

"That's it," said John. "He had a core gun, a hollow tube piercing the bloomin' roof and taking samples!"

We looked at each other in amazement. I asked, "How come the rain hasn't leaked through?"

"Because that's a false roof," John explained. "The Bibles are in there."

On the evening that had been planned for us to meet our contact, we had to unload the Bibles without being seen by the guard. The job of the women was to cause a distraction by chatting and laughing loudly as we washed dishes outside the caravan, whilst the men loaded the Bibles into the boot of our car. John had instructions to drive slowly down a particular street. When it was safe to do so, a man would walk out of a house and jump into our car.

Sure enough, a young man suddenly opened the rear door of our car and leapt in the back, sitting right next to me. I could feel him trembling with fear as he gave instructions to drive quickly down the street.

"Go! Go!" He looked over his shoulder nervously to see if we were being followed.

"Turn the car around!"

John made a U-turn, screeching the tyres.

"Take a left, then right! Right again!"

This went on for some time until he was satisfied that we were in the clear. My heart was pounding as we sped round the city. There was a moment when I thought, "I am out of my depth; this isn't an action movie – this is for real! What if we are being tailed by the secret police? We'll be arrested, interrogated. How do we explain our real purpose for being here?" I felt the proximity of the fearful young man next to me. "Is he married? Does he have children? Is he known to the KGB? Have they got their tabs on him – will he go to a labour camp? Will he die?" My heart was breaking. I tried to pray, think of Scripture, but it was useless. All I could think of was this young man risking his life.

Eventually we left the wide city streets and began making our way through lots of narrow passages. Tenement blocks towered over us, grey and forlorn in the fading light of day.

"Stop!"

John slammed on the brakes and, as we came to a sudden halt, he inadvertently touched the car horn. It blared loudly. This is not a great thing to do when you're trying to avoid attention, but the young man remained still, watching.

"OK, get out quickly!" John lifted the bags from the boot, handing them to his fellow "smuggler", and the two companions followed the young man through a battered door. Their footsteps echoed and vanished.

The wind was blowing down the empty street as we women sat silently praying. Our plan was to act as if we were lost, with our crumpled map at the ready. Ten minutes seemed an eternity to us. At last, the two men reappeared and got into the car without a word. I wanted to ask questions, but no one spoke.

As we gathered our courage, ready to leave, another young man stepped out of the shadows. Our eyes met for a second. Was he a lookout? Was he friend or foe?

There was something about his piercing blue eyes and his strong presence that burned into my soul. Perhaps he was the pastor of the fellowship… Whoever he was, I could hear the words echoing: "It is finished." The mission was accomplished and the silent figure, gazing at our departing car, was filled with joy.

Later that evening, John said to me, "Rose, I have to admit that I was ill-prepared for what we have just experienced. Do you remember, back in the 1970s, how you would go to Thursday family Bible study at the home of Max and Howell Jones? I saw a change in you then. You seemed so much more confident and self-assured. You kept harping on about Jesus 'being alive', His Spirit 'living in you' – you were going on and on about God's grace and how much He loved you."

"Yes," I said, as the memories came rushing back.

"Frankly, I didn't get it. I was happy for you, of course, but all that stuff… Well, it wasn't for me. But just now…"

John was deeply moved and, for once, very serious.

"Just now, in that tiny room in the tenement building, there was something… a look in the eyes of the old man, the joy on the faces of his family. They didn't have many possessions, hardly anything, but they had love… they had so much love, in abundance. I've never seen anything like it. Sheer joy… and hope… in the middle of all that poverty and darkness and fear."

My eyes filled with tears at John's description of those remarkable Christians. John was welling up too.

"I felt peace… that peace Jesus talks of."

"Peace that passes understanding…"

"Yes… you can't explain it; you can only experience it. And that's what happened to me in there."

I was in no doubt that this was a very important moment for John.

"I am convinced", he continued, "that we made the right decision to come on this trip – particularly me. I believe that you and I are being tested for some greater purpose."

Our homeward journey gave us lots of time to reflect on the past weeks and, above all, on the change in ourselves.

Ringing my sister Lynne from a roadside telephone box in Finland (no mobile phones in those days, remember!) was fantastic. I was so happy to hear that my darlings Ju and Steve were fine. Lynne was very relieved to hear my voice and to be assured that John and I were not spending the rest of our lives in the Siberian salt mines.

I love Lynne, so straight-talking – the one who always sorts me out. "I bet you're dying for a decent cup of tea," she said. I'm grateful that Lynne and Keith took such good care of our children whilst we were away and for the many faithful friends who were holding us in their prayers throughout our journey.

An adventure like this seems a little incredible now, since, only a few years after our trip (in 1989), the Iron Curtain came down, the Soviet Empire collapsed, communism lay in ruins, and millions of Christians and peoples of other faiths found freedom for the first time. But sadly, as I have already said, there are more Christians being persecuted and martyred in the world today than ever before. We should cherish our freedoms in Britain and stand up for freedom of religion throughout the whole world.

There is one little "PS" to this story. On our return to the Open Doors headquarters, we went for a debriefing session – and they were happy to know that it was a clear case of "mission accomplished". However, Miss Marple (aka Rose) was eager to find out whether the secret password for entry into the workshop was changed for each assignment.

"What secret password?" our bemused colleague asked. To which John Lancaster – looking at me with that all-too-familiar expression on his face – confessed: "Sorry, Rose. Knowing how much you like a bit of intrigue, I only wanted to encourage you…"

I gave John a severe look and he burst out laughing. "When you saw that ship, 'Flying Goose', you were so excited about God giving you a sign that He was with us. Well… I hadn't the heart to tell you that I had made it all up!"

My husband is such a rogue. But I like to think that it was a genuine sign, not only that God was truly with me, but also that He has a wonderful sense of humour. After all, he created John…

Well, enough of exotic adventures in Russia; it's time to get back to business in Clitheroe – although, as you will see, our so-called "normal life" was about to become crazier than anything we had ever imagined.

CHAPTER EIGHT

Explosion!

Many people have asked me about the secret of John's success in business. Perhaps they are hoping for a magic formula or some golden rules that they can follow. There are, of course, many characteristics that I can point to. He's always inquisitive, has a great sense of humour (as we have seen!), is full of self-belief, communicates his ideas with great passion, is very resourceful, and is determined to turn technical problems into great solutions. He won't take "no" for an

Ultraframe large span conservatory roof.

answer, but he is not proud and listens carefully to advice. He is extremely hard-working, and inspires others to follow his example, but he is also very compassionate and ready to give people a second, a third, a fourth chance, as long as they are prepared to work hard too. He really believes in his employees and has always been prepared to go the distance in order to get the very best out of someone. I sometimes think that his experience of bitter failure, bullying, and despair at school, ironically, has been a great advantage. He understands struggle and does not want anyone to give up on themselves. He is always full of hope.

Well, that's quite enough praise for my husband, especially as it comes from someone who knows his weaknesses and shortcomings too. John and I try not to cherish too many illusions about ourselves, and the fact is our success has a great deal to do with the ultimate model of business success, which you can read about in the Gospels. It comes from grace and it comes from the only perfect human being who ever lived – and He taught us that our lives are only truly successful if we love others as much as we love ourselves.

The president of a US marketing business, Laurie Beth Jones, has even written a remarkable book called *Jesus, CEO,* and this puts into words many of the principles of leadership and business success that John and I discovered, often through hard experience, as we stumbled along the winding path to the climax of the flotation of Ultraframe on the stock market in 1997. In this passage, she perfectly sums up something that we came to realize was perhaps the most important principle of all:

A speaker from Dallas, Texas, recently shared this story with members of the National Speakers Association. One young man, set to run in a one hundred meter race in the Special Olympics, had trained for months and months. But when the gun finally sounded and he leaped out in front of the rest, it seems the excitement of the race overcame him. Each foot went in different directions, and the well-meaning athlete came tumbling down right in front of the starting block. The other racers, each as eager as he was to compete in this great event, nevertheless stopped running their own race and turned back to help him. The crowd came to their feet as his competitors lovingly lifted him up and then walked arm in arm across the finish line together.

These runners in the Special Olympics made me think of Jesus and his set of rules. I thought about him choosing to tell the story about the shepherd who cannot rest as long as even one sheep is still missing, despite the ninety-nine of them which aren't… about a father who is waiting on the road, watching for his lost son to come home, even though he has one son who is serving him ably and well… about a king holding a banquet, who will not start serving dinner until every place is filled at the Great Table…

And I wonder what this world would be like if we played by that rule: that nobody wins until we all do.

I am so thankful that we came to understand and truly experience this in our factory in Clitheroe. I knew I had been called to be "Aunty Rose" and that this sometimes meant being marriage guidance counsellor or agony aunt as well as making the tea. It meant learning to look out for everyone else, even when it was tempting to put ourselves first. I'm sure we made lots of mistakes, but, as time went on, we saw the whole workforce responding to a culture of belonging. They shared the challenges and they shared the successes. Ultraframe was a family, with a strong identity.

We made the highlight of every year the annual "bonus evening". Our business was the first company in the north-west to establish a PRP (profit-related pay) bonus scheme, which has significant tax advantages for the employees. These bonus evenings were held just before Christmas. It was a time when we shared our vision, inviting employees to talk about their experiences too.

Bonuses of over 20 per cent of annual pay became the norm at the height of our success, and it was thrilling to see the joy and power of this encouragement for many people who had experienced very little in the way of exciting holidays or material comforts in their lives. We felt very deeply that this business belonged to everyone who had contributed so much. We organized a great Christmas meal, we had live music, and John would make people laugh with his stories and his off-beat observations about life. He was always full of ready wit but, much more important, he was overflowing with encouragement.

It's amazing and very sad how discouraging many workplaces and corporate environments can be. Nothing can grow in such unpromising soil. The special culture that existed in Ultraframe was almost tangible – you could see it in the smiles and in the commitment and in the environment of friendship. This powerful and very productive quality was widely recognized in the industry.

John and I both realized that when you strive to do the best you can for people, the best is what you get.

"Nobody wins until we all do."

This is one of the greatest principles to live by, and it still remains at the heart of everything we do. Jesus, the most brilliant "Chief Executive Officer" who ever lived, put it another way: "Love your neighbour as much as you love yourself." There's a lot of talk about love in the world; millions of songs, stories, adverts, and films proclaim the glories of love: "Love is all you need", "Love makes the world go round", "Love me tender, love me true"… But what *is* true love?

It is very rare to hear any song about love that mentions the word "sacrifice". But if we are meant to love other people as much as we do ourselves – if this is what makes us truly human and lifts us above selfishness and fighting for our own interests all the time – then we need to be able to let go, to be giving, and to be prepared to make sacrifices for the sake of a higher good.

Looking back, I realize that sacrifice was a very important part of the process for us. We had to live simply, forgo a lot of comforts, and put up with very long working hours, endless disappointments, setbacks, and all the ups and downs of a risky business, and, gradually, we had to learn to put our growing workforce before ourselves, just as good parents put their own children first. This was never easy and we had a lot of growing to do, psychologically and spiritually. We're still growing and learning every day.

The Jewish Talmud says, "Every blade of grass has its angel that bends over it and whispers, 'Grow, grow'."

I love that picture, and it's a beautiful aid for me when I pray for my precious grandchildren. "Grow, grow…"

They are all growing physically, with dramatic differences every year, but there are other areas of growth that do not happen so naturally. They must be worked at. Some people think that maturity and wisdom occur automatically. As you get older, you get wiser. I can tell you that some people in their fifties and sixties are a lot more stupid now than they were at fifteen. They have let selfish ambition, craving for money or sex, lying, bitterness, or hatred take hold of them completely, binding them like some kind of poison ivy. Anyone who is completely self-obsessed is also extremely immature.

John and I pray that our grandchildren will grow in every way, in character and in spirit, and we hope that they will all increasingly discover the meaning of true love, which certainly involves some sacrifices along the way…

And many risks too.

One of the things I have learned from John (I hope he has learned from me too!) is his capacity to make mistakes. Yes, you read that correctly. Mistakes can be creative!

John's view has always been that it is better to try something and fail than not to try at all. Making mistakes is often how we gain knowledge and develop character. He says firmly that no one should ever buy into the philosophy of "If I can't do it right, I won't do it at all". Because almost everything we do is done imperfectly at first. John worked for many years, tackling numerous types of business, learning important skills that would later serve him well as an entrepreneur. Success did not come at all easily, and it came after a journey of many risks, failures, and mistakes.

It is difficult to comprehend John's pain after failing his 11-plus exam, but at the time it felt so final. It looked as if the word "Failure" was emblazoned on his forehead: he was a "loser", a "failure", a "no-hoper"… he would go nowhere. He would do nothing worthwhile in his life. The truth has been the complete opposite of this, and his many mistakes in the exam and his awful disappointment at public failure lie at the root of a very determined character.

The American Quaker poet John Greenleaf Whittier (1807–92) wrote:

Many a failure turns about
When he might have won if he'd stuck it out.
So stick to the fight when you're hardest hit
It's when things seem worse
That you mustn't quit!

OK, it's not Shakespeare, and this budding poet might have failed his 11-plus too, but it makes excellent sense to me. It's another of the great principles of life.

Well, I've cantered off in another direction from the main story of this chapter, which is the explosive success of Ultraframe. But it's all because I want to put this in context. No one should be dazzled by the figures that follow, or make too big a drama out of material success, without understanding the human story and the long personal learning process that has been involved for both of us.

One mistake that John didn't make – thank goodness – was to succumb to a tempting offer of £60 million from a national company for Ultraframe in 1995. It was a difficult decision – yes, we would have been on easy street financially – but John's instinct was to turn it down; he believed, and took the risk of his belief, that Ultraframe was worth far more and had a significant future. But his chief concern was that the company making the offer could not guarantee that Ultraframe's employee benefits would be retained. And that was completely non-negotiable. John stepped back from the instant "now Rosemary and I can retire comfortably" temptation, the short-term gain, for the sake of a long-term vision.

Once again, he was living out a crucial principle: take the long view. This is important in difficult relationships and life challenges, as well as in demanding business decisions. Going for short-term gain often leads to trouble and disillusionment.

Over the years, Ultraframe expanded rapidly until it became one of the largest employers by far in the Ribble Valley, vying with Castle Cement to be the area's largest industrial employer. They were also looking to develop an export market to the US, Canada, and Europe. By 1990, the company was listed in Moneymaker magazine as seventh out of the two hundred fastest-growing companies in Britain.

In 1991 we were thrilled to win the prestigious Lancashire Rural Business of the Year award, and two years later we had a wonderful tenth-anniversary celebration for the whole workforce. By now, you will have realized that we love parties... and we were soon to have the most amazing party of all.

In 1996, Ultraframe started preparations for flotation on the stock market, an incredibly complex and arduous process. There was masses of paperwork, along with meetings and high-level consultations in London. Everything was looking really good for Ultraframe as it moved towards that all-important transition from being a privately owned company to becoming a publicly listed company, owned by thousands of shareholders, on behalf of pension funds, investment banks, and large numbers of ordinary investors and speculators on the stock market. We wanted our entire workforce, now numbering 550, to own shares and we wanted to give them away free. This was truly a moment when everyone, the whole Ultraframe family, had to share in the excitement and prosperity. Our financial advisors insisted that everyone had to buy shares for a token amount, to make everything legal and official.

John laughs now at the memory of people who were not sure about making this purchase... He even ran seminars so that people who did not understand about stocks and shares could understand what they were doing. Some tough-minded Lancastrians were determined not to be deprived of their precious pounds in this strange and unfamiliar world of risky enterprise! But John, of course, was very persuasive.

He organized a special bonus for all employees so that they could afford them!

We also included many sub-contractors in the special share offer, and decided to write cheques to compensate the considerable number of employees who joined the company after the share issue, so that no one felt left out.

The great day came in 1997. John was whizzing all round London in a taxi, going from one financial institution to another, one bank to another, to verify the incredible reality that was now unfolding…

I began the book with this story, but I hope you won't mind my repeating it – because the whole event is still like an amazing dream to me. As you know, I could scarcely understand all the financial processes, but I can say that Ultraframe was admitted to the London Stock Exchange with "an initial market capitalization" of £136 million, with each share valued at £147.

I was in Clitheroe at the factory. John telephoned me from London with the flotation share price and I was in such shock that I got everything wrong as I relayed the information to the puzzled employees.

"It's £136,000," I mumbled.

"No, no!" John was hollering on the phone. "*Millions.* It's bloomin' millions, Rose! One hundred and thirty-six million pounds!"

I looked at the enquiring faces of the workforce. "Um," I stuttered, "it's, er, actually one hundred and thirty-six million pounds!"

The place went wild. People were shouting, cheering,

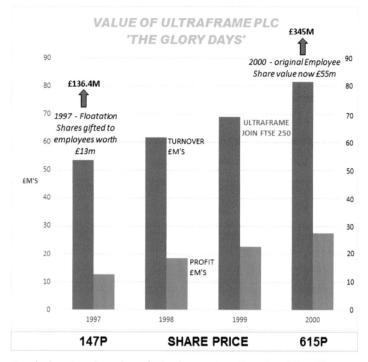

VALUE OF ULTRAFRAME PLC
'THE GLORY DAYS'

£345M

£136.4M

1997 - Floatation
Shares gifted to
employees worth
£13m

2000 - original Employee
Share value now £55m

ULTRAFRAME
JOIN FTSE 250

TURNOVER
£M'S

PROFIT
£M'S

£M'S

| 1997 | 1998 | 1999 | 2000 |

| 147P | SHARE PRICE | 615P |

Graph showing the value of Ultraframe since flotation. We still pinch ourselves today, asking "Did this really happen?". (Orange = turnover and blue = profit, both in millions.)

laughing, dancing… they soon had their paper and pencils out to do some calculations. On average, our workforce made £20,000 each on that day… and, in a very short time, this amount doubled and tripled.

The truth is, we gave away £13 million to our employees on that day, because we felt very strongly that this was what God had told us to do. He had blessed us beyond our wildest dreams, but He hadn't blessed us for our own sake. And we knew that He had a purpose behind this staggering windfall, which was meant to bring healing, hope, and joy to many people. In the very instant of our astonishing good fortune, we knew that a profound responsibility had come to us and, in many ways, our lives had prepared us for this.

But today was a day for a massive party!

John struck the right theatrical note by flying back from London in a helicopter and landing with his two fellow directors near the massive marquee we had erected next to the factory. I'm surprised the downdraught didn't blow cream cakes into everyone's faces, but nobody would have minded. The whole experience was like a crazy dream, full of laughter and happiness. Our friends Ray and Nancy Goudie had written a special song to celebrate the moment and they performed it live. It was an instant hit, of course, with an admiring workforce who were already totally euphoric. John gave every worker a CD and told them to play it in every pub and club.

Another great friend of ours, Jilly Farthing, was in on the celebration. She remembers the day vividly: "We filled my little Peugeot car with balloons and I drove round Clitheroe with Rose's sister, Lynne, and her husband, Keith. The town was full of merriment. We went to the Key Street Club and played the CD, dancing and whooping. The regulars got fed up with hearing it and sloped off home! Then we all went off, with John and Rose, for a celebration dinner."

It was celebration from morning till night, and for days and weeks to come. The money that came to hundreds of local people had a significant impact on the economy of Clitheroe, as other businesses benefited from people decorating their homes, buying new furniture, arranging holidays, etc. We were thrilled that this was not some kind of isolated "rich man's fantasy", but a genuine experience of communal blessing. (Clitheroe is very important to us: we grew up there, we have always lived there, and part of our dream now is to continue to enrich the life of the community there – another chapter to come!)

But at this incredible moment of rejoicing, in the middle of 1997, all I could do was hold my breath and think, "Flippin' 'eck! What next?"

John, Rosemary, Julie and Steven at the North West Business Awards.

CHAPTER NINE

The Lancaster Foundation

Next came all the accolades. Awards poured in for John because of his entrepreneurial skills and innovative designs. We attended lots of business functions in London and awards evenings and exhibitions at home and in Europe. However, many of these occasions took me out of my comfort zone.

John's wit and sense of humour served him well as a

Leaflet promoting "Venturer of the Year" award.

speaker. He was brilliant at captivating his audience. People truly respected him, and I must say that all the attention he received made me very proud of him. I knew what this journey had cost and how long it had taken, from such an unpromising start in life. We were astonished to find ourselves meeting many important and famous people, in politics, industry, and entertainment, but I'm not going to start name-dropping now – I've never liked that habit in other people! But we were certainly riding high. We were a couple of swells, staying in the very best hotels. However, I was never happier than when returning to my wonderful family in beautiful Clitheroe.

Many times when John has spoken, he has attributed his success in business to our relationship. "Behind every successful man is a good woman" has been one of his favourite sayings. I have always liked the comic version of this, which goes, "Behind every successful man is an astonished mother-in-law." But I know that my mum, who always believed in John, would have been just as thrilled as I was. I really wish she had been around to see how things unfolded, but who knows? Perhaps she was, in some special way.

There is a deep truth in what John says, though, because no one is really an island. The Bible tells us that two people working together in unity is a cause for rejoicing, and three people bound together in a common purpose – the "threefold cord" – is even better. We all need encouragement and support. We need each other, and so the best relationships, friendships, and partnerships often lie at the root of the greatest business successes, the most powerful films and artistic achievements, the most important social reforms and political campaigns. Relationships of love are often at the heart of success.

Supporting John, and working very hard with him, was natural for me, and I am so glad to have played this part. I'm not sure that in an age when everything focuses on the individual – "find yourself", "discover who you are", "live your dream" – that we make enough of "supporting roles". Perhaps there's a little bit in each of us that wants the "Best Actor" Oscar rather than "Best Supporting Actor". We want to be in the limelight, to be the centre of attention, and, in the words of the Frank Sinatra song that is played at far too many funerals, we want to do it our way…

I don't really like the selfishness that has come to be almost admired in our culture. I am glad that my role has been one of supporter, companion, and encourager. There is nothing wrong with this and, of course, it is a two-way process in a good marriage. Husband and wife must truly support each other and believe in each other and make space for each other.

Well, John was giving me lots of credit and space and taking me with him everywhere. Hard work never bothered me, but meeting strangers at posh dinners was a nightmare for me. It may not always seem like it but my natural character is really quite shy, and these functions were sometimes rather a torment to me.

I would find myself trapped between clever financiers and investment bankers and I would be grilled about Ultraframe's growth plans and future strategy. I don't think the reply "Yer wot, luv?" was an appropriate response, but it was often what I was thinking. I can't say I was either interested in the business complexities of the conservatory market or knowledgeable about any of the financial details of the company. So I developed a cunning plan: *distraction.* Or, as the cowboys used to say in the old western films, "Let's head them off at the pass." I would ask men about their families, their wives and children, their own childhood and upbringing, and, sure enough, they would talk happily about themselves for ages! This was how I used to get off the hook, but my strategy failed on one occasion.

John was a finalist for the "*Financial Times* Businessman of the Year Award", held at the glittering Grosvenor House Hotel in London. I was sandwiched between two very sharp investment whizz-kids. They had no children and no interest in children and were obviously completely out of touch with their own childhood and upbringing. No! Money, in all its shapes and forms and infinite possibilities, was their only subject, their obsession, the altar at which they worshipped. As I was not a fellow devotee of money and I had no desire to worship with them, nor could I string two sensible sentences together about fluctuating interest rates or the benefits of hedge funds (which I assumed were something to do with gardening), I was completely at a loss. When one of them talked intensely to me about investing in American companies, I foolishly murmured something about having "seen an article in *The Sunday Times*", which they seized on, only to find that I hadn't really read it. My heart was pounding with embarrassment and I mumbled meekly, "Oh well, you'd better talk to my husband."

I'll probably get a severe lecture from any radical feminists reading this, for having given the worst possible answer in the history of women's liberation: "Er… talk to my husband." My dinner companions were not impressed and turned to the people on their other side. I was blanked for the rest of the evening.

The good bit about this nightmare story is that John won the award. He was given a beautiful pen, a black leather wallet, and a Cartier watch. In his speech to the great and good (and not so good) who were assembled there, he paid tribute to me and his wonderful employees, and thanked his family for all their love and support. I was a key to his success. From feeling utterly inadequate, I suddenly felt uplifted and truly valued. The following day there was a full two-page feature on business entrepreneurship in the *Financial Times*, including a large photo of me! There was John, too – the "Cartier and *FT* Business Venturer of the Year".

The success story of Ultraframe continued. The late 1980s and early 1990s had been a time of recession, but despite this gloom the UK conservatory market was flourishing. All sorts of people, including politicians and industry leaders such as Frank Dobson, Gordon Brown and Paddy Ashdown, had come to Clitheroe to try to discover the secrets of this success. The truth was, John hadn't just stumbled into a growing market; he had actually made it happen. The period from 1988 to 2003 saw the industry grow from 25,000 to over 300,000 conservatories at its peak, with Ultraframe achieving an amazing 60 per cent of the market share of the supply of the roof systems that they had invented.

Eventually, the business became the largest employer by far in the Ribble Valley, with a local workforce of some 800 people in the UK, plus another 400 in the USA and Canada, and a thriving export market in Europe.

That's as far as I can go with numbers and figures (which John has given me), as my head is already spinning and, as I have already said, these great figures – £136 million, £13 million, 60 per cent market share – should all be seen in context.

Our life is not about impressive figures. It's not about money. I hope you know by now that it's about people. And the first thing we had to do, as soon as the wild partying and heady days of euphoric celebration were over, was to remember that we had been called to a higher purpose and to act out of sheer gratitude.

Here we were with all this wealth, a local boy and girl from Clitheroe, and we really had to keep our feet on the ground. But this wasn't easy, when John bought a high-tech helicopter! It caused quite a stir in the town, taking off and landing in our garden, but over the years it proved invaluable for John's business and visiting our UK charity projects. It was great fun and many of our friends and family were sad when we finally sold it, many years ago.

However, the way to keep our feet truly on the ground, in those heady days, was to look outwards, not inwards. After the flotation, we transferred a substantial shareholding into the Lancaster Foundation. We were complete novices at any kind of organized charitable enterprise, particularly on such a big scale, and we both knew that we needed a director whom we could really trust.

There was one very special local friend, one of the most important people in our lives and a true extra member of our family: Jilly Farthing. We thought she was perfect for the job, and John approached her.

Here's how Jilly remembers that moment:

My three brothers and mother had emigrated to Australia and I was at a crossroads wondering whether to join them or stay in Lancashire, where I had so many dear friends. For three years, I had wavered over this decision, but I had finally made the choice not to settle in Australia – at the very time John and Rosemary were going through the mammoth decision of how to preserve the success of Ultraframe and the well-being of its workforce, whilst liquidating a significant part of their interest in the company in order to form a registered charity.

The timing was perfect, because I had returned from an exploratory trip to Australia now determined to stay near Clitheroe, give up teaching, and go back to college to freshen up my typing skills... I had no idea what lay ahead. I volunteered at the Women's Centre in Blackburn, contemplated the future, and prayed... but the future was still a blank.

That's when John gave me a letter in his own hand, which I still have and treasure. John is a man of a great many talents, but writing is not his favourite occupation...

The letter is a very special souvenir of what I can only describe as an extraordinary answer to prayer. The gist of it was, "Would you like to join the Lancaster Foundation as its first director? An office building has already been bought, Text House, just near Throstle Nest. Rosemary and I think you will be great for this post."

My head was reeling and my little local prayer group were amazed that somehow, and so soon, God had provided a tailor-made job for me. I immediately knew it was right.

We were very happy when Jilly agreed. We trusted her and loved her and knew she was ideal for the job. She was also great fun; there was plenty of laughter whenever Jilly was around. As far as John and I were concerned, this was the number-one qualification!

Text House is called this (long before the advent of mobile phones) because it has a large biblical text carved in the stone wall at the main entrance. Soon John, Jilly, and I were trying to imagine – and start to manage – all the incredible potential of this Foundation, which would have its home in this lovely building. Back to Jilly again:

As soon as a trust is formed and publicized on the Charity Commission's records, it is inundated with requests for funding. Hundreds and hundreds of brochures, accounts, personal letters, and appeals came through our letter box. We had no idea that so many charities existed even in the UK. Our statement was just too general – "Christian work"; we had to be selective and we had to know where to begin.

And, at the same time, I felt strongly that we needed to keep the whole world in view.

This brings me to the text in the wall. It's probably the best-known text in the whole Bible, and it comes from the words of Jesus in chapter three of John's Gospel (NKJV):

For God so loved the world that he gave his only begotten Son, that whoever believes in him should not perish but have everlasting life.

Here is the supreme example of love and sacrifice being truly one and the same thing. Jesus was talking about giving His own life up for the whole of humanity.

Considering such a gift to the world, the greatest gift of all time, setting up our charity was just a very small act of pure gratitude.

We believed that God had blessed us richly and now He was giving us the greatest privilege of all. He was calling us to share our life, and our good fortune, with others.

CHAPTER TEN
Flying High – MAF

John and I hung a map of the world on our wall. It was a simple gesture but it felt like the beginning of an epic space adventure, with the pounding drums of the theme from *2001: A Space Odyssey* playing… something amazing was about to happen to an ordinary couple from Clitheroe!

We looked at each other. "Where do we start?" We had a few pins on our map but no idea what to do next. We

MAF plane "Leader" at Borama.

prayed that God would reveal His plan for the future and guide us in our decisions.

It is an astonishing thought that any man, woman, or child can make contact with the Creator of the universe. It's also a sad thought that many people think prayer is unimportant, neglect it, take it for granted – or, perhaps worst of all, think prayer is only for their own needs and comforts. Of course, we had both made many of these mistakes ourselves in the past. But, from now on, John and I realized that we had to pray more deeply for the needs of the world, because we had been given a very great responsibility. We knew that we were stewards of God's money and our task was to serve the poor and needy, to honour our commitment to share God's heart wherever we went.

It felt as if the world map on our wall was staring back at us. There were thousands of needs and worthy causes, and it seemed impossible to know where to begin. I remember Mother Teresa being asked by a journalist: "How can we change the world?"

She replied, "One person at a time!"

But which person? And where?

I could never have imagined the impact of our simple prayer on that day: "Please guide us!" This was the beginning of a journey of discovery, a trip deep into the heart of Africa where we would encounter situations that I could only dream about in my fanciful years as a child.

God certainly listens to the prayers and longings and even the impossible dreams of children… and this is why I am telling you the amazing story that was to set the scene for so many adventures and surprises that changed the lives of countless people, including myself.

The ancient Chinese philosopher Lao Tzu is quoted as saying, "A journey of a thousand miles begins with a single step…" And we were about to take our first step.

Bob Edwards – our financial advisor – came across a leaflet for MAF – the Mission Aviation Fellowship. He knew that John was very interested in flying machines of all varieties: helicopters, planes, microlights! So Bob passed it on, confident that this unique story would appeal. It certainly did. The story of MAF captured John's imagination.

At the end of the Second World War, a number of airmen in the UK, USA, Australia, and South Africa all began to wonder how they could use their experience for the benefit of the world in peacetime. They had survived the horrors and constant dangers of warfare, but it seemed that God was calling them to draw deeply on their expertise and courage to reach out to the poor. Amazingly, this calling came to several people in very different countries – "Let's use small planes to bring help to needy people in remote places in the world" – but the idea soon gathered momentum and a number of Christian pilots, leaving their national air forces, teamed up to form the Mission Aviation Fellowship. MAF UK and MAF USA were both established in 1945. These were the first two groups to start operations and were soon followed by MAF Australia.

According to the leaflet, the first three operational groups

all had very small beginnings. Each lost an aircraft early on. Each learnt many lessons flying in remote

MAF PRAYER DIARY

PRAYER WAS THE ANSWER THEN, PRAYER IS THE ANSWER NOW

In 1945, Murray Kendon one of MAF's founders wrote 'Gather into a prayer fellowship as many as possible who are vitally interested in the hastening of world evangelisation by the use of the aeroplane.'

Since the beginning of MAF, prayer has been foundational.

The call that Murray made all those years ago has been answered. For 70 years we have had the joy of partnering with passionate people who call out to God on MAF's behalf. People who trust in His faithfulness and the power of prayer.

Again and again we've seen God's mighty hand intervene with miracles of provision and protection.

Thank you for praying with us. We rejoice at seeing God's will being done, His love shared with some of the world's poorest and most isolated communities, and countless lives transformed for eternity.

Please join with Stuart King, another of MAF's founders, whose prayer for the next 70 years is:

'Lord, keep us in Your will, help us to live for Your glory – help us to make sure You are first and not the work. Raise up people who will be better than we ever were – more skilled, more in love with You and still pioneering!'

Let's keep praying!

*regions and difficult terrain – mountains, jungles
and swamps… but today, MAF has grown to a
worldwide fleet of over 135 aircraft operating in more
than 30 countries. From its small and struggling
beginnings, MAF has expanded into a highly developed
organisation. God has done great things.*

John perused every word of the brochure, learning about
relief flights in Ethiopia, operations with relief agency
Medair in north-east Somalia, and the missions during the
terrible Rwandan crisis of 1994–95.

Losing no time, he asked Jilly Farthing, the new director
of the Lancaster Foundation, to make a phone call to MAF
headquarters. Before we knew it, Howard Morgan, head of
fundraising, was sitting in our lounge.

Howard Morgan is an extraordinary man. His profound
deafness has not prevented him from travelling the world
and raising lots of money for different organizations. He was
soon sharing the vision of MAF very powerfully and he told
us of the desperate need for a new Cessna aircraft to increase
the capacity of this amazing work.

John listened attentively, and then asked Howard, "Is this
what you really need?"

Howard nodded, "Well, yes…"

"If resources were no problem, what would you really
want to purchase for MAF?"

This was new territory, even for Howard. People did not
normally ask such bold questions about the ideal scenario.
Most donors are content to make a reasonable contribution to

the immediate needs of an organization. He swallowed hard.

"Well, this would do us well," he said, pushing a leaflet for the Cessna to one side. "But there is another option." Slowly, he reached into the slim briefcase at his side and pulled out a brochure for a Pilatus aircraft. "It seats twelve people, and has the capacity to travel much further than the smaller Cessna but on the same amount of fuel. Payload is excellent. The plane flies greater distances without refuelling in dangerous zones. It's remarkable." Howard was clearly on a roll. "Excellent night instrument flying; only short airstrips required; it can easily land on rough ground…"

"I like the sound of that," John interrupted his flow.

"It has many other superb features –"

John glanced at me. I could see his excitement. He didn't need to hear any more and we both looked at each other. His heart and mine were completely at one.

I will never forget Howard's expression when John said, in a very matter-of-fact way, "Let's go for it."

There was a long silence.

For a moment, taking in the immense shock on Howard's face, I thought that the fundraiser from MAF might need an MAF plane himself to get him quickly to intensive care… But he soon recovered, and his joy was indescribable.

Jilly Farthing was a witness to this moment, and here are her own words:

I was in complete shock when John suddenly said, "Let's buy that one!" Howard was stunned. He was utterly speechless. Who were these people? It takes years of meetings, charity fundraising events, promotions, appeals, unbelievable patience, and endless grind, to raise that amount of money, and here was a couple who hadn't even discussed it between themselves. Just a look from John to Rose and that private language that only a loving couple know. Rose simply agreed with him, without saying a word: "Let's buy it!" All those years and years of stress and hard work and anguish; this was the moment when it all becomes exquisite. It was thrilling to see this happen.

And why Howard had the brochure for that dream aircraft in his bag, when MAF was fundraising for a Cessna, who knows? He certainly had no idea that such a dream could come true in a single second.

But what an incredible opportunity – to bless this charity, and one that blesses umpteen other charities by flying personnel across Africa or South America or wherever, taking wounded and dying people to hospital, saving so many lives. John and Rose had bravely seized this opportunity, and this was just the beginning.

Before long, John and I were on our way to a factory in Switzerland to see the plane being assembled. Then we had the thrill of watching her on her maiden flight. I must confess that we were in love with an aircraft! And we loved being in partnership with MAF.

The following year, Jilly, John, and I joined Howard on a trip to MAF's centre of operations in Nairobi. This was the first of many trips to Africa. I could hardly believe that I was on my way. My youthful dream (an impossible one, I had thought!) was finally becoming a reality. As the plane roared along the runway at Heathrow Airport, images from the film *The Nun's Story* flashed into my mind, and in less time than it takes to make a day trip to the seaside at Morecambe in Lancashire, which had seemed a fabulous distance when I was fourteen, we were flying over Africa.

As I gazed at the vast continent below and the River Nile, like a green snake sliding through the barrenness of the desert landscape, I wondered how people existed in their tiny villages and raised their families in such unforgiving conditions.

Eventually, as we flew over Kenya's capital city, Nairobi, my eyes were drawn to Kambi Teso slum, a vast sprawl of makeshift shacks and humanity crammed together like ants in a nest. It was a vivid contrast to the shining commercial centre, with its tall buildings and streets jammed with traffic, and the outer suburbs with their affluent homes.

Following a good night's rest, we were very excited to attend the official ceremony for the new PC-12 in MAF's hangar at Wilson Airport. My heart was bursting with joy as I feasted my eyes on the beautiful plane. I climbed the steps and entered the aircraft and there, on the left, I noticed two plaques with these words: "Dedicated to our beloved grandson, Joshua Benjamin Broadhurst: 'Be bold, be strong, for the Lord your God is with you!' Joshua Ch. 1."

Joshua was a great leader in the Bible and it was only fitting to call the new plane "Leader", because it opened up brave new horizons for the great work of MAF. And I like to think that my eldest grandson Joshua is a leader too…

Rosemary with Joshua, our eldest grandson.

Now an eighteen-year-old, going off to university, he is highly-valued, talented and skilled, a fine young man who still has the capacity to melt my heart when he says "Love you, Gran"...

Howard insisted that we went on safari, but never again! I was stricken with "African tummy". There were wonderful sights to see, but I was frequently hiding in the toilets, wherever I could find them. I don't think I would have made much of an addition to a David Attenborough documentary: "And so, from morning till night, we hear the familiar groaning of the Tourist in the Toilets, a very common sound on African safaris..."

As we were in Maasai Mara land, Howard insisted that we visit a camp of the famous Maasai tribe. Eating just small amounts of boiled rice gave me enough strength to make it through the journey to the Great Rift Valley, where they live – part of a huge canyon that stretches three and a half thousand miles from Syria to Mozambique. The Maasai warriors are a proud tribe of hunters. They cut a cow's neck vein and catch the blood to drink – not a sight that was calculated to make me feel any better. It is said that even the lions don't go near them, and I can't blame them, because of the terrible pong from blood and milk mixed in the same containers.

We bought a few trinkets of jewellery that the women had made. It was all so surreal to me: crocodiles sunning themselves by the river, acacia trees, hippos roaring in the distance, wild animals prowling around everywhere, like a scene from *Out of Africa*.

I certainly felt I was in a dream, or a movie – but at least, if you are watching a movie, you can rush out to the ladies at any time. This experience, of incredible beauty and exotic animal life, mixed with rather basic human anguish, is burned into my memory.

But I do remember some very amusing things from that trip. A morning cup of tea and a biscuit were left on our veranda early in the morning, but we had to take them quickly before the monkeys swung by and ate everything. I have often referred to John as a "cheeky monkey", but even he was never as cheeky as this! Then there was the time we saw an amorous male ostrich chasing a very unimpressed lady ostrich… the gentleman ostrich was very determined but his efforts were completely doomed. It reminded me of that scene in the film *Dumb and Dumber* when Jim Carrey asks a beautiful girl what the odds are of her going out with him. She looks at him sternly. "I'd say about a million to one."

Jim Carrey smiles, undaunted, and says, "So you're saying… there's a *chance*!"

I noticed how the elephants would get very cross if we came too close in our open-top jeep, but we didn't go near enough to discover exactly *how* cross elephants can get… I'm a very curious person, but there *are* limits. I also didn't want to give myself too much of a fright, for obvious reasons.

On our fourth day we returned to Nairobi, where we met a pastor and his wife who were working among the Maasai people. They arranged to take us with them to a village. It seemed to take a lifetime, travelling slowly along rutted mud roads, with giraffes trotting alongside us. My tummy was still very queasy and I felt every bump and swerve in the road. I remember thinking of the lives saved by MAF, who are able to fly sick and injured people directly to hospital. So many people have been spared agonizing days of travel on rough tracks, invariably carried by relatives or pushed along in hand carts. At least my own relatively trivial suffering increased my sympathy, and my admiration, for MAF.

At last we arrived at the village, which consisted of round mud houses, surrounded by a fence of thorny branches to keep the goats in and the wild animals out. The chief, who was a convert to Christianity, welcomed us into his home. It was dark and smoky from the fire on the ground. The chief sat on a wooden cot, holding out his hand and smiling, showing a set of worn brown teeth. He wore traditional red dress, a small band around his head, and a necklace with a huge animal claw or tooth attached (it was difficult to make out through the smoke). I was relieved not to be offered a drink, as it would have been insulting to refuse their hospitality. So far, I was surviving all right, and I didn't want to push my luck any further!

As we left, we noticed his two wives giggling with lots of children around them. The children looked at us hopefully. We were soon playing football with them with plastic bags squashed and tied together into a squidgy ball! It brought back memories of days in Clitheroe when we all played endlessly in the cobbled streets with a few makeshift toys or a battered old and punctured football. In some ways, life was much simpler then in England, as it was now in this African village in 1997. Amidst all the deprivation and poverty, there was great fun and laughter and community – both in the Clitheroe of my childhood and especially in this remote village in Kenya. I sometimes wonder if our modern world of very expensive toys and gadgets, and obsession with computer games is any real kind of improvement. We take so much for granted today in the Western world – not least being able to watch films at the flick of a switch. It's so easy that we become almost bored and blasé about everything.

John and I were about to witness a community that took none of the marvels of modern technology for granted... After dark, the whole village gathered with great excitement as a screen and a big projector were set up by the pastor and his wife. The projector was connected up to a car battery. They showed the *Jesus* film to about fifty villagers – men, women, and children, sitting on the ground. The crowd were held in rapt attention. They laughed, they cried, they cheered when Jesus performed a miracle! It would be hard to find that kind of spontaneous joy in a typical Anglican church in England – we've got far too used to these extraordinary gospel stories. Perhaps we've tamed them and we keep them in a zoo called "church services", when they should be roaming free in our imagination, like the wild animals on our African safari.

That night, John and I received a lesson in simple and beautiful and powerful response to the Bible. Every twenty minutes, the reel finished and had to be replaced. During the five minutes that it took to put the next reel on, all the villagers stood singing and dancing and worshipping God. My heart was melting with such wonder at these beautiful people, with their simple faith and joyful faces. But when it came to the crucifixion, the villagers groaned with anguish, they wept at the fate of Jesus, they sobbed at the terrible injustice. Then, gradually, they dried their tears as they experienced the wonder of the resurrection morning with its great hope for the future and the glorious truth that Jesus was alive for ever. Once again, the villagers were on their feet, singing and dancing and celebrating with all their hearts.

They had found true riches, far greater than any of the material success that John and I had experienced in our lives. We were very deeply moved. To be honest, it is impossible to be the same again after seeing the gospel received in this way. Jesus Himself said, "Blessed are the pure in heart, for they will see God" (Matthew 5:8, NIV). And I think that we came to understand a little more of the beauty and truth of the Beatitudes in that Maasai village: "Blessed are the poor…

blessed are the meek… blessed are those who hunger and thirst for righteousness…"

We were blessed by the Maasai people, blessed by the faithfulness of the pastor and his wife who had dedicated their lives to sharing the kingdom of God with this tribe of proud warriors. And we had been blessed by MAF and our great good fortune in becoming involved in supporting its work.

Over the years, it became possible for us to increase our commitment to this amazing worldwide ministry – we were able to help purchase and dedicate two more planes for MAF. The 22 December 2000 was a memorable date for us, because it was the birth of our second grandchild, Madelaine Esther. She was a great joy to her proud parents, Julie and Philip. I can only describe Maddie as the best possible Christmas present! Beautiful inside and out, she has an aura of peace surrounding her. She has grown up stable and dependable, with a wonderful spirit of service, and so the plane called "Esther" is fittingly named after her. Many lives throughout southern Africa have been blessed as this special plane continues to provide emergency relief during crises, bringing medical supplies, and transporting missionaries and doctors and food during times of famine.

Not to be outdone by her older sister, Julie and Philip's third child, Tilly, now has her own MAF dedication too. Tilly was born on 10 November 2003 and soon we were able to make a substantial contribution towards another plane. Tilly is a gorgeous girl, inquisitive and a real character, with an air of mystery – a bundle of energy; an amazing dancer

Our grandchildren Tilly, Josh, Maddie and Levi – to whom the planes were dedicated.

Our daughter Julie with her husband Philip on their wedding day – their children were those to whom the planes were dedicated.

and gymnast. I like to think that her plane has a special sense of adventure, bringing love, relief, and practical support, this time to the people of Madagascar. I can't help thinking of the plane doing aerobatics, a bit like Tilly in the garden at home! We chose a verse to be inscribed in this plane: "Your love, Lord, reaches to the heavens, your faithfulness to the skies" (Psalm 36:5, NIV).

It's a very rare privilege to be able to include our grandchildren in the worldwide adventures that have been unfolding for us. Needless to say, with regards to MAF, we were always receiving a great deal more than we were giving. It was a wonderful first step for us.

And I can truly say that, from the moment of our first trip to the Maasai tribes onwards, Africa was in my soul and the people of Africa were in my heart.

CHAPTER ELEVEN
African Adventures Continued

We soon found ourselves swept up into a series of African adventures. I can honestly say that these amazing experiences changed John and me more than they did anyone else.

There is a wonderful image that I believe comes from St Teresa of Avila, a sixteenth-century Spanish nun who had many adventures of her own. She talks of the "exchange of

"Traffic congestion" in Borama, Somaliland.

hearts", which is a very beautiful way of understanding prayer. God says to a man or a woman, "Give Me your heart, with all its longings, its troubles, its worries and desires, and I will look after it. I will provide for all your needs. I will cherish your heart, and in return, I will give you My heart, with all My love and longing for the world. I want you to carry My heart within you, and love others as I love them. I want you to love the poor and the broken of the world as passionately as I love them. You must feel My heart beating inside you."

It's the case for most of us that our longings and prayers tend to be focused on ourselves, but God wants to change all that. And this was what He was doing to John and me, through a very different kind of African safari. We were not tourists, out to see the sights and have a great holiday. We were pilgrims, being taken on a journey of spiritual transformation by God Himself.

Soon after our first MAF trip, we joined the Christian Blind Mission team, headed by Dr David from the UK. We boarded "Leader" again in Nairobi for a two-hour flight to Borama in Somaliland, a town of 25,000.

It is hard to imagine anyone living in such a desert region. Suddenly, small white houses came into view below and soon we were landing on a narrow airstrip. We were greeted by a string of dignitaries and split up from each other as we were swept along by their enthusiasm to see us. It felt as if we were being kidnapped by strangers – but it was a very friendly crime! The intense heat in the air and the burning sand nearly overpowered me and I was glad to finally make it to our hotel.

We were assured that this was the best accommodation in town. It took the form of a small room with two single beds with hard pillows and mosquito nets. There was a dusty dining room with a wooden veranda where we ate a simple meal, but we were glad to hide under our nets and escape the mosquitoes. We felt like two small children in a dormitory at some curious boarding school. When we put the lights out the darkness was intense, and we were whispering to each other a little nervously and laughing. John seemed too far away from me and the night sounds were overwhelming. There was the occasional raucous screech of some bird – or was it a hyena? – and the buzzing of insects and the chafing of cicadas filling the air. It can be quite unnerving for English people – Africa is very noisy at night!

In fact, John was so unsettled by the feeling of a world out there, seething with exotic and potentially lethal bugs and dangerous creatures, that he had a dilemma in the middle of the night. He was bursting to go to the loo, but the loo was in a nearby building… John decided on the lesser of two evils. He took the option of utilising a plastic bag, a manoeuvre which required night vision and accurate aim. I'm glad he achieved this successfully, because otherwise it might have been like that famous scene from *Scott of the Antarctic*, when Captain Oates leaves the tent with the words, "I may be gone for some time" – and never returns. I didn't want to find John's bleached bones in the desert, with some very fat bugs and mosquitoes burping nearby.

After breakfast in the morning, we joined Dr David for his remarkable eye clinic. To coin a phrase, this was truly an "eye-opener" for us, as well as for his patients.

We were escorted to the surgery by the minister for tourism (though who on earth would choose this place for a holiday?), down a sandy road and past the ruins of concrete buildings and the rusting machinery of some failed US military mission.

It's hard to describe the conditions at the hospital, a group of single-storey buildings in the midst of this bleak and desolate scene. There was no glass, just empty window frames, and concrete walls that were stained and dark. Various rooms had been prepared as theatres, but they were only just big enough for a bed and a trolley with instruments. John and I had been asked to attend the operations and help in some simple ways. I should say that our Foundation director, Jilly Farthing, was with us on this visit to Borama, but she decided to stay safely away from the eye operations. The very idea of such surgery was already making her feel squeamish! She volunteered instead to direct patients in and out of the theatres.

Rosemary and Jilly with young nurses at Borama hospital.

Dr David and the other two surgeons, with the help of a few nurses, conducted over 300 cataract operations in three days. Many people, both young and old, had travelled miles by foot over sandy and rocky terrain to reach Borama. Families had escorted blind relatives, hoping desperately for a cure. A great crowd was sitting all around the hospital buildings, waiting to be seen by the miracle-working doctors. It could have been a scene from the Gospels. It was easy to imagine Jesus walking among the longing people, touching, healing, loving, blessing… And Dr David and his colleagues were really like that: ambassadors from heaven, representatives of Jesus on earth.

Meanwhile, John and I were floating on the edge of this sea of desperate humanity, proudly wearing our theatre gowns – and frequently being mistaken for doctors. People were showing us their eyes, hoping for healing. John was certainly very good at nodding at people and smiling reassuringly. I was really loving my role, helping the patients as they were given a local anaesthetic injection in the corner of the eye and then escorting them into the theatre. The patients were fully clothed, except for one old man who had only a loin cloth and a gnarled walking stick. There was no air conditioning and the temperature was in the thirties. The plastic green theatre beds needed constant wiping down because of the perspiration.

A dignified Muslim man walked in and I helped him, as politely as I could, onto a bed. It was clearly very difficult for him to come there, but he had been driven by desperate need. It was a challenge for me to accept the cultural rule not to speak to him or touch him with a reassuring hand. It's natural for me, as you may have guessed, to put a hand on someone's shoulder, or put my arms round them when they are obviously distressed. I was learning to do this in my imagination, through prayer and by just being present, in a more humble way.

Swiftly, the surgeon made a small incision in the cornea with a small section of a razor blade. Other instruments had been sterilized over a flame burning from an ether bottle. Gradually, he removed the opaque lens, replacing it with a new clear lens ($7 each), with a small stitch to hold it in place. I covered the eye with a wad of cotton wool and secured it with sticky tape. I helped to lead the man into a ward crowded with people, where he recuperated for two days. On the third day (saying this seems very reminiscent of Easter), the dressing was removed.

You should have seen the joy on his face.

Over and over again, this procedure was followed with hundreds of people, but it was always the removal of the dressings that had such a memorable impact. There was one twelve-year-old boy who laughed when he saw Dr David's three fingers – and counted them correctly. His beautiful smile will remain with me for ever.

The gift of sight… we so often take this for granted, but no one healed in this way will ever do so. Of course, there were often people who could not be cured, because they were suffering from inoperable blindness, and, at moments like this, faced with such severe disappointment, I longed for Jesus Himself to walk right into the room and say, "Receive your sight!" However, as medical science keeps on developing, perhaps more and more people will be helped to receive their sight in the most dramatic ways by the "flying doctors" of the MAF, and by the numerous missionaries, doctors, relief workers, and angels of mercy at work in the world.

The hospital at Borama was like a sign of hope, an oasis of joy and potential in the desert of human suffering. Healing is very much in the heart of God for His beloved children in this world, a truth which I hold on to, even when so many still suffer and so many appear beyond healing. We must never give up praying, serving, loving, and doing our best to make a difference, however small it is.

One evening some time later we dined with the medical team and met an amazing lady, Dr Annalena Tonnelli. She had been working in Somalia for thirty-five years, since the country had gained independence from Italy. Everywhere we went, we met such wonderful angels of love and compassion, people who had lived lives of continual service and sacrifice. It made us reflect deeply on our own lives, and our own culture, which can seem so shallow and materialistic. Yes, through such amazing people, our hearts were being opened wider and wider.

But as always, in the middle of great and serious matters, there was plenty of room for laughter. One of the MAF pilots was describing a rescue mission to a flooded village. His co-pilot noticed a large woman stranded in a tree. He tried to grab her hands as he leaned out of the helicopter, to heave her up to safety, but she was far too heavy for him.

The recovery ward at Borama hospital.

As a result, there was a complete reversal of the normal rescue attempt: he fell out of the helicopter and landed on top of her, as she straddled her legs across the tree branches. Luckily, no one had a camera handy to photograph this compromising situation: "Christian Pilot Shares Intimate Moment with Woman in Tree". They were both winched to safety, and a discreet veil was drawn over this incident.

Talking of compromising incidents, John was soon involved in another one. MAF took us to an amazing place called Beautiful Gate, an orphanage in Lesotho which cares for abandoned HIV babies. Youth With A Mission (YWAM) runs the home with support from the MAF pilots' wives.

We were greeted joyfully on our arrival, offered refreshments, and then treated to a special dance by the young Lesotho women. They honoured John by giving him a Lesotho crown and cloak. This encouraged John (never a shrinking violet) to join in the fun enthusiastically. He started to dance and laugh with one of the women, and this led to all the dancers falling about in absolute hysterics. John had unwittingly taken part in a tribal love dance. Apparently, when a Lesotho girl reaches the age of sixteen, she is then ready to entice a young man to marry her. Part of her ritual dance involves the impressive skill of making her breasts swing around in opposite directions – this is a sure sign of her fertility. The young man who responds with suitable enthusiasm to her enticement then becomes her husband.

No wonder everyone laughed at John's response – unknowingly he had offered himself in marriage and found a second wife: "Christian Businessman Caught in Bigamous Love Triangle"…

John and Rosemary in Lesotho.

Despite these bizarre and comic beginnings, this little AIDS orphanage, caring for about twenty babies, planted the seeds of one of our most precious adventures in Africa.

We were soon supporting a Salvation Army home for AIDS orphans in Soweto and this was how a very special woman called Corinne McClintock came to hear about us.

I can honestly say that this "chance connection" (I don't believe in chance!) led to one of the most important things in the whole story of my life: Sparrow Rainbow Village in South Africa…

CHAPTER TWELVE

Sparrow Rainbow Village

Corinne can begin this remarkable story in her own words:

In 1989, the AIDS epidemic hit South Africa and dealt a heavy blow to the poor, who were then treated as the lepers of the modern era. I am a Professional Registered Nurse who became very concerned about this problem.

I had led a chequered life and was still nursing, whilst

Sparrow Rainbow Village.

attending a Bible college at Rhema Church. I was not sure what I wanted to do with my life, so I decided to fast for three days. God gave me a message that was inspired by the prophet Isaiah: "Do not fast but take into your home those who are cast out; be a light to the nations."

I was living in a small house, still at college and attending lectures, when a friend told me about a Salvation Army lecture on the disease known as AIDS. I went along to a really poor area called Mayfair, where they provided a soup kitchen to which people with AIDS came along. Rhema Church also wanted to set up a counselling centre for people with AIDS. I visited another place called the Sacred Heart House, started by a paramedic who was a sufferer of AIDS himself, where AIDS patients were cared for. I saw the compassion and got involved. This was in 1989.

It began with opening my little house to three guys whom I could care for, but then a friend gave me a larger house to accommodate more AIDS patients. Three or four miracles happened; people gave money.

I had a dream of the ideal houses I would want for the AIDS patients to live in and I even drew a plan. Others were coming to me all the time – a mother and child turned up on my doorstep. I knew that something bigger needed to happen and I took my AIDS village plan to the social services. There was one guy there who was interested and he took it to the council, who were prepared to give me land.

At this point, St Gabriel's Church in Florida started an AIDS group and they came to visit my house. Among them was a lady called Valerie Carter, who said, "I have a friend in

Clitheroe who is very generous, and she may help you." So I gave her the business plan with some photos. Valerie visited the UK to stay with her mother, and took my information to Rosemary Lancaster. Rosemary told Valerie how they were already supporting the Salvation Army counselling centre in Soweto and that they were soon coming over to visit it. Rosemary took my leaflet home and was astounded.

By the time they came to visit, we had been going for over six years. I was now discussing the shape of the houses for the village and a woman took me to see an amazing dome house that had been created by a builder from the Cape called David. Dome signifies "House of God" (from the Latin *Domus Dei*), but it was also very practical, low-cost housing. The hole in the top of the dome functioned as vital air conditioning, and this was essential, as AIDS patients often develop TB – all the bacteria could escape through the hole.

John and Rose walked into my life just as the dream of the AIDS village was being born… and just at the point when I knew that, although land had been offered, there were no resources to make the dream a reality…

I can't begin to describe my own emotions on first meeting Corinne and visiting her home, which had been opened to so many suffering people.

It really was like entering the heart of God.

I was overwhelmed by this wiry sixty-year-old South African lady, whose passion was infectious. It's easy to forget that, in this world ravaged by disease and death, there are some infections that are truly spiritual and positive.

I caught the vision.

Corinne's house had three bedrooms full of beds and cots; even her lounge was full of beds. She lived in a small caravan in the garden, whilst caring for more than twenty people who were HIV-positive and destitute.

I saw a young girl, eighteen years old, blind, emaciated, her body ravaged by the relentless disease, her immune system no longer able to fight off the infection. My heart broke as I pictured a beautiful girl dancing and enjoying life, imagining one day becoming a professional dancer. This had been her dream. I looked into her unseeing eyes and was filled with a sense of rage at the huge injustice. It was all too cruel.

The babies in there tore at my heart. I held on to one baby, near death, with no strength to suckle. I asked Corinne how many she had lost.

"Follow me," she said, and we went into her garden where there was a large tree. "There!" she said. Nailed to the tree were tiny brass sparrows, each bearing a name. Corinne's beautiful memorial broke my heart. I promised her that these little ones would never be forgotten. "I tell them all about the Lord," she said softly; "how He watches over every one of us. His eye is always on His sparrows." The verse from the Gospel came instantly into my mind: *"Are not two sparrows sold for a penny? Yet not one of them will fall to the ground without the will of your Father"* (Matthew 10:29). The tiniest birds are precious in God's sight, and every little detail of our lives matters to our heavenly Father: *"Even the very hairs of your head are all numbered. So don't be afraid…"*

Looking at this tree, full of shining sparrows, I began to sob uncontrollably. I had seen for the first time the results of the HIV/AIDS pandemic and the tragic premature loss of life. And, through Corinne's inspirational love and compassion, I had been allowed to see into the heart of God's love for His beautiful little ones. Every single life and death is precious in His sight.

This was no ordinary encounter. I knew that our meeting would be significant.

Corinne was an expert in her field of nursing and pastoring destitute and dying people. Her medical training and her studies for ordination had come together in the most powerful and radical form of Christian love: it was simple, it was practical, it was right there, literally on her doorstep, in her home, in her garden... in her mind, heart, and soul. I felt that I had touched a blazing fire of love.

Later that evening, she began to share her vision with me. Years ago, she had had a dream. She was walking down a road. She suddenly turned and saw a crowd of toddlers in nappies walking towards her. She wondered in amazement at all these babies. Was she going to be a mama? Babies desperately need support, someone to love them and hold them and feed them – but how could she care for so many? The AIDS pandemic was spreading rapidly. Corinne urgently wanted to find a safe place for all these babies. She then told me of some land where she wanted to build a village, where people could live out their fragile lives as normally as possible.

Corinne grew excited, sharing her dream of becoming self-sufficient, growing vegetables, teaching skills, making jewellery, selling to local communities. She was going to build a church with rooms for a Sunday school, a hospice, children's homes with play areas, laundry and kitchens… I could hardly keep up with the flow of her ideas, which were tumbling out with such love and enthusiasm!

"Have you found the land?" I asked.

"Yes," she said. "As a matter of fact, I have looked at six possible parcels of land! But you know, Rosemary, I prayed to God asking Him to guide me to the right plot of land. He said to me, 'Taste the grass; it will be sweet.'" Corinne was always full of surprises – and full of fun. I looked at her, astonished, laughing, imagining her chewing on lumps of grass, while sheep and cows looked on, very puzzled. "What's this weird human being doing grazing in the field?"

Corinne was laughing. "Yes – I tasted the grass. And the grass on the last piece of land was sweet!"

That's how she had found the site for her village.

I loved this crazy lady from the first moment we met. I looked at her weather-worn face, her eyes glinting with mischief. "Corinne – I like what you are doing!"

The rest is history: Sparrow Rainbow Village… Let Corinne continue in her own words again:

Rose said, "I like what you are doing!" and John said, "How much do you need?"

I said, "Eight million South African Rand" (about one million pounds sterling).

"OK," they said, without blinking, "we'll give you four million SAR."

They had absolute faith and trust in me. I was dumbfounded.

With help from other sources too, we set about building the first AIDS village in the world – a light to our nation in the darkness of AIDS.

It was 1999, and Jilly Farthing and I flew out to Johannesburg to visit Sparrow Rainbow Village for the first time.

I was full of excitement and joy at the thought of seeing the reality of Corinne's wonderful dream and meeting the many precious children in her care. Jilly was excited too, but her feelings were mixed with considerable trepidation. She had read too much about attacks and assaults on women after dark in Johannesburg.

"Oh, we'll be fine," I said, as the lure of another great "African adventure" took hold of me. I couldn't wait to get there. Corinne picked us up at the airport and then drove the forty minutes to Sparrow Rainbow Village. She explained to us that the security fence was not complete yet, but her faithful security guard would be on watch all night. "Although," she added, a little mischievously, "his sight and hearing aren't so good."

Jilly nearly passed out with fright.

We arrived in near-total darkness, except for a few lights shimmering. My first impression was of "Tellytubby Land", with all the dome-shaped houses. I expected "La La" or "Tinky Winky" to greet us warmly, but this thought did not cheer up Jilly. Corinne was making things worse by regaling us with a typical story of life on the edge of the townships: "By the way, last night a group of men attacked our project manager with a machete, but I fired my gun in the air and they quickly scarpered. He had a gash on his head that I had to stitch, but he'll be OK." Now I was beginning to lose my adventurous resolve. "Well," said Corinne cheerfully, "do sleep well; I'll see you tomorrow."

"Sleep well"? Hardly. "I'll see you tomorrow." Was this a normal goodnight courtesy, or an act of faith? We did *not* sleep well… I can tell you that every little sound outside that night had Jilly and me hiding under the covers!

But our first, mostly sleepless, night was soon forgotten when we met the children in the morning. Corinne had lined them all up and they sang us a song of welcome. Although many looked sick, with swollen tummies, we were captivated by their gorgeous smiles. Their welcome was truly heartfelt, rousing, and deeply moving. It was hard to imagine that some of these little ones had been abandoned at birth in rubbish bins or latrines, or even left to die in disused mines. Their struggles and indeed their lives are a million miles away from even the most difficult circumstances that we see in the poorest areas of England.

It's easy to feel inadequate, to ask "What can I do?", in such extreme circumstances. It's true that John and I had been able to give significant financial support (only because of the grace of God in our lives), but this story is not about money. Anyone can show love when they encounter suffering, and I learned at Sparrow Rainbow Village that very small gestures mean a very great deal. Perhaps this truth is most obvious when there are no cures and people of all ages, especially the very young, are facing death all around you.

Rosemary with some of the children at Sparrow Rainbow Village.

"What can I do?" The answer is, do *something*; do whatever you can.

I had the great privilege of spending many hours, day and night, with a little girl called Juliet. She was only eleven years old. Perhaps I was too optimistic, hoping that she would somehow pull through, and I was encouraging her to eat and not give up. I spent a lot of time reading and singing to her. My privilege was to be on her journey with her, and her journey was ultimately a short and peaceful walk into the embrace of God Himself.

It was incredibly moving to stand beside that little grave, freshly dug, with its simple wooden cross and the inscription "Juliet – aged 11 years". All around were tiny graves, many with babies' bottles, toys, or clothes decorating them, and simple messages. I witnessed plenty of tears and deep grief in those days. So many of Corinne's little sparrows too weak to go on – yet more victims of the cruel injustice of AIDS.

In the months and years to follow, we were able to help a lot of young people, especially students at New Generation Music and Mission (NGM) in Bristol, to come out to Sparrow Rainbow Village and experience the tragedy and the beauty, and the great love of Corinne and all those working with her. These visits profoundly affected the lives of the British young people, whose eyes were opened to the suffering in God's world. A very beautiful song was composed and sung about Juliet, and the singer Tanya was filmed singing at her graveside: this became the end piece of the musical *Luv Esther*, which toured the UK.

Luv Esther was a very special project, and in many ways it was inspired by the vision of Sparrow Rainbow Village and the call to compassion and strong action across the world. I'll tell you more about it in another chapter.

Right now, my mind returns to one person in particular, who has a very deep and secure place in my heart.

She was called Primrose.

Corinne had asked me to take my guitar into her ward and sing to her. They were concerned that she had given up and was refusing to take care of her son, Shepherd.

Primrose lay very still, thin and gaunt. Her face was beautiful. I sang a hymn, and then sat down beside her bed. I noticed a Bible on her cabinet and asked her if she would like me to read her something. Slowly, she raised her hand and nodded. I asked if she had a favourite passage and she whispered, barely audibly, "Psalm 91." I began to read the words, addressing them to her:

She who dwells in the shelter of the Most High
  Will rest in the shadow of the Almighty.
I will say of the Lord, "He is my refuge
  And my fortress,
My God in whom I trust…"

You will not fear the terror of the night
  Nor the arrow that flies by day
Nor the pestilence that stalks in the darkness
  Nor the plague that destroys at midday…

"Because she loves me," says the Lord, "I will rescue her;
  I will protect her, for she acknowledges my name.
She will call upon me and I will answer her.
  I will be with her in trouble
I will deliver her and honour her."

Psalm 91 (NIV)

I noticed out of the corner of my eye that her lips were moving. As I finished the passage, I said, "You know the words?"

"Yes," she replied. Then she began to tell me her story.

"I was married to a wonderful man. I loved him. I was training to be a pastor, but then my husband died. In my grief, I reached out for comfort from my tutor and we slept together, just one night, and I got pregnant.

"And I contracted AIDS.

"Now I am dying. My family have disowned me. Who

will take care of my little boy? His name is Shepherd, because I want him to be a leader."

I asked her if I could visit her the next day. She agreed. To my surprise, she was sitting up in bed, watching her son lying at her feet, his clothes wet and smelly from an overfull nappy. I got clean clothes and washed and changed him.

Primrose was fascinated by the baby wipes. She loved how nice he smelled as she cuddled him. We talked for a while and then prayed together.

The following day, Primrose's bed was empty. The nurse told me she had rallied, asked for her clothes, got dressed, and was sitting outside with the other ladies.

Jilly and I painted their nails, massaged feet and legs. The gentle touch of another human being was pure medicine to the patients. We laughed and sang together.

My final visit was one of joy mixed with sadness. I had grown so fond of Primrose. We sang "Amazing Grace" together, her expression telling me that she meant every word she sang.

As I left, so reluctantly, I glanced back. Primrose waved her thin arm in a gentle farewell. She was still smiling and singing.

I would never see her again.

Three weeks later, I received a letter from the Village: "This is to let you know that Primrose has died. Just before she passed away, she said, 'Will you write to Rose and tell her that she put a song back in my heart? I'm ready to be with Jesus.'"

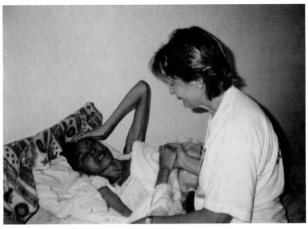

Rosemary with Primrose.

I wrote to Corinne on the eve of Primrose's funeral and this is the full text of my letter:

Tuesday 9 April 2002

Dearest Corinne,

I have just been watching the Queen Mother's funeral on TV, very poignant and moving, lots of dignity and ceremony – extremely fitting for such a remarkable lady. An estimated 400,000 turned out to bid their own personal farewell to the nation's Queen Mum.

During the service at Westminster Abbey, my thoughts constantly turned to Primrose and her funeral to be held the following day, which will be in very different circumstances. And yet, realizing in death we are all equal in the eyes of God, we are as one.

I remembered holding Primrose in my arms and marvelling at her deep faith and trust in God who loves unconditionally, and her confident Amen in response to the amazing grace of God.

There is a lovely flower that grows under hedgerows and on grassy slopes, waiting for the warm, spring sunshine to draw its beauty out of the cold, dark earth of winter – turning its delicate yellow petals towards the kiss of the sun.

A primrose.

During the winter of her life Primrose blossomed in a beautiful way; she reached out to the warmth of the Son, claiming her inheritance in Jesus, her Saviour. Though I knew her only briefly, her life has impacted me very deeply – "God has done a wonderful thing for me" (Luke 1:49).

Your eye is a lamp lighting up the whole of your body – if you live wide-eyed in wonder and belief, your body fills up with light. (Luke 11:33–36)

You and Primrose have opened my eyes to see the wonders of God's creation and the joy of giving in His marvellous service – in a new way. I still feel full to overflowing.

Another tribute to the Queen Mother came from the words of George Eliot:

Like the sun she bathed us in a warm glow.

May I dedicate those words to Primrose – a friend of only a few moments – until we meet again in glory. I will be thinking of you tomorrow, and pray for God's peace as you commit your precious flower into His loving care.

I see myself now at the end of my journey
My toilsome days are ended
I am going now to see that head
That was crowned with thorns
And that face that was spit upon for me.
(The Pilgrim's Progress)

Love as always.

Lots of hugs,

Rosemary

As I look back on the life-changing adventure of Sparrow Rainbow Village Ministries, I am full of gratitude. First of all, that time has moved on and, with advances in medical science, there are now far better antiretroviral drugs and treatments available, offering significant hope to many. But I am truly grateful for the continuing witness of Corinne, a shining light, who has kept faith with her vision and her God. She has brought life to people not just physically but spiritually – she has raised many to spiritual life, even as they

Rosemary and John with Corinne in front of a list of donors to the Sparrow Rainbow Village.

lay at death's door. She has given hope against impossible odds. She has opened windows into heaven and the true, eternal nature of God's healing love.

And I am most deeply grateful that John and I have had the chance, through Corinne, to make a difference. But, as I have said many times already, the biggest difference has been in our own hearts. We cannot be the same after such experiences, nor can we be so obsessed with ourselves and our own small world of wants and needs. Sparrow has helped to liberate us, and has also shown me the incredible power of dreams.

When I was fourteen years old, I saw the film *A Nun's Story* and I dreamed that one day I too would help children in Africa. (I was going to be a nun as well, but, fortunately for my children and grandchildren, that part of the dream didn't happen!)

But as a girl I dared to dream… and the dream that I would play a part in such loving and caring for children thousands of miles away from my own home town came true.

Any boy or girl, man or woman, has the potential to make many wonderful discoveries in life, and none greater than when they explore the truth about God – and themselves.

> *The pursuit of my dream has taken me out of my comfort zone, elevated my thinking, given me confidence, and confirmed my sense of purpose. My pursuit of the dream and my personal growth have become so intertwined that I now ask myself, Did I make the dream or did the dream make me?*
>
> John Maxwell, *Put Your Dream to the Test: 10 Questions that Will Help You See It and Seize It,* 2012

Looking back, John and I have realized that our greatest joy was not in the goal we reached but in the growth we experienced on the way to it.

So, my advice to my grandchildren and everyone else reading this book, young and old, is: dare to dream. Enjoy the pursuit of your dream. And be prepared to change, sometimes in wonderful and sometimes in painful ways, in living out that dream. Be prepared for a life of spiritual adventure.

CHAPTER THIRTEEN

Two Projects in the UK: The Story of NGM and The Message

"Dare to dream" – these three words sum up the incredible faith adventure of Ray and Nancy Goudie, two of our greatest friends. Their life and work had such a deep influence on our family that we eventually became involved in a major UK arts project called New Generation Music and Mission (NGM). We came to see, through the work of Ray and Nancy, that there were huge needs on our own doorstep.

In the nineteenth century, William Booth, the founder of the Salvation Army, wrote a book with the provocative title *In Darkest England and The Way Out* (1890). He was reminding his Victorian readers, who were giving generously to African missions, that there were great social problems in their own society – staring them in the face, if they would only wake up and pay attention! The Salvation Army became renowned for reaching out to the poor and needy, but William Booth is also famously said to have asked, "Why should the devil have all the best tunes?" His army

Ray and Nancy Goudie.

marched around the towns and cities of Britain literally banging drums and playing wonderful brass-band tunes and melodies. It was gospel music before its time, jazzed-up hymns, full of joy and power, far more rousing and inspiring than some of the hymns being sung in parish churches.

Now, in the twenty-first century, church leaders sometimes talk of a "lost generation" when they look at their empty pews and see young people queuing outside nightclubs, listening to the latest hits on iTunes™, or watching the latest pop videos on YouTube or MTV.

Ray and Nancy understood this split between church culture (some people call it "Churchianity") and popular culture better than anyone I have ever known. When I first met them they were members of a successful band called Heartbeat. They had an international reputation and a song in the charts; they looked stylish and glamorous, they were funny, and they had faith!

John and I were in awe of their impact on our own church, when they came to run a mission in Clitheroe. Our own children, Steven and Julie, were teenagers at the time and they were mesmerized. This was different: they hadn't seen anything like it before. Thrilling pop music, dance, laughter, celebration, passion… Ray and Nancy seemed to live out the miracle of the wedding at Cana, when Jesus saved the whole party by turning 120 gallons of water into the best vintage wine. I have heard well-meaning people argue that the wine might have been non-alcoholic... 120 gallons of Ribena? I don't think so.

There is a deep cultural crisis in Britain, where there is a desperate need for the power and life of the Christian gospel. One of the first things John and I experienced with Ray and Nancy was their impact on a teenage audience, especially our children. And it wasn't just in their performances, because Ray and Nancy also showed such love and kindness to us as a family. Ray spent many hours, many sessions, teaching Steve to play the drums. Years later, Steve would join Ray and Nancy down at NGM in Bristol and it was a life-changing experience for him (not least because he met his wife, Anna, through one of his NGM friends!).

Steven and Anna on their wedding day.

But one of the other things John and I experienced with Ray and Nancy, from the beginning, was their wicked sense of humour.

One of the times I can truly say I have laughed most in my life was at a posh hotel, where Ray and Nancy were our guests. We knew that they "lived by faith" and had very little money, and we wanted to give them a treat. We had an excellent meal but, at the end of it, Ray noticed the couple at the next table get up and leave.

"Look," he said, his eyes sparkling, "they've left more than half a bottle of wine!"

"Ray, don't get any ideas," warned Nancy, as if anticipating what was to come.

Ray looked around furtively. He then got up, laid a white napkin over his arm, and transformed himself into a wine waiter.

"A little more wine, madam?" he said to me, and started to flounce around the table, seriously overacting the part, and pouring out the expensive vintage wine for Nancy, John, and finally himself. Then, leaving a small amount in the bottom, he placed the bottle back on the neighbouring table.

By this time, several other guests in the dining room were riveted by Ray's performance. Meanwhile, Ray relaxed, smiling, savouring his extra wine – but suddenly his satisfied expression changed to horror. The neighbouring guests had come back into the dining room and were returning to their table. It was clear they had just been outside to have a smoke!

We were crying with laughter as a variety of tortured expressions passed across Ray's face as he waited to see if they would pick up their bottle. Amazingly, they didn't notice, but they were certainly puzzled by the hilarity in the dining room, which now included several other tables of guests.

The incident was so vivid at the hotel that, the following morning, the waiters and waitresses begged us to tell them what had caused all the laughter. Luckily for Ray, they hugely enjoyed the joke.

Well, that was rather a diversion from my story, but it does illustrate something important: laughter and celebration are infectious.

So are love and faith.

Ray and Nancy's incredible dream was to share the new wine of the kingdom by creating a pop academy for young people, which would train a new generation in the highest levels of singing, composing, recording, dancing, and performing. Their vision was to bring together the technical arts of sound recording and music production, using the best possible studio resources, with voice training, artistic direction, and choreography. All this was to be bound together in a communal life of worship, living faith, and spiritual development. They wanted their young musicians and performers to engage with the local area through projects of service and social action, mission, and evangelism.

It was truly a great vision and, as is so often the case, it started very small.

First, there were offices and a studio in an old barn in Malmesbury. After many years, there was a home at the Bristol Christian Fellowship, which gave NGM the use of a building in the centre of the city.

I'll let Nancy describe some of the adventure in her own words, from her book *Hot Faith*:

> *After being in Bristol for some time, we felt it was right to begin to pray and ask God for premises of our own. After some weeks of praying, Ray and I felt God say to us that He was going to give us a missions and arts complex. We knew we were in for a big walk of faith; little did we realize what a huge walk of faith we were embarking upon. We thought we were praying to God to supply around £200,000 in order for us to buy a house in which we could have our offices and perhaps change the garage into a studio. We were thinking small. God, however, was*

thinking big. Our journey of faith led us to believe God not for £200,000 but for three million pounds.

If we had known at the beginning that our missions and arts complex would have cost £3 million, I am sure that our faith walk would not have started. God knew that it was best to let us know the information bit by bit, and as we trusted Him for one bit of the plan, He then led us to the next part. One thing I have discovered throughout all our walks of faith is that God is wise and He knows our frailties. Right at the commencement of our "journey" God told us "not to worry about the money but birth the project in prayer." It was good that He said that, because at that precise moment in time, we did not have one penny towards our faith goal…

But one night, Ray and I received a phone call from two of our close friends who told us that they had heard from God. They wanted to give us a donation towards our "Caedmon" project (this project was named after Caedmon, who was a Celtic Christian bard who lived in the Dark Ages and was known for writing songs that reached into the culture of that day). We were excited and very encouraged. We weren't sure how much they would give, we thought perhaps a few thousand pounds, but when we heard that the "donation" was a very substantial sum of money, we were overwhelmed.

We first met John and Rose over thirty years ago, when they were living in a caravan with very little. They were generous to us then and have continued to be so to this day.

To be honest, John and I had been overwhelmed by the love and generosity of God – not just in the fortune made on the flotation of Ultraframe, but in our daily experience of forgiveness and joy – and so we were thrilled to be in a position to overwhelm someone else with that same love and heavenly good fortune.

I remember John commenting drily, when Ray first talked about NGM, "What does NGM stand for, Ray? 'Not Got Money'?" Ray and Nancy were the first people we knew who genuinely lived by faith, and this was very mysterious to us! How does that work? We had known what it was like to live on the very edge in the past, but to *choose* to do this, every day of your life? Two well-educated and talented people, called by God and living by faith – and giving their heart and soul to create wonderful opportunities for young people, artistically and spiritually? This was amazing and impressive to us and we heard a clear call from God to play our part.

To hear Ray and Nancy talk of the journey towards the whole development of the NGM Caedmon complex in Thornbury was inspiring. There were many ups and downs, huge highs and lows, crises over property sales and sellers changing their minds, the threat of planning permission being turned down – endless obstacles that would have defeated people of lesser faith and courage.

As we travelled on the long journey with Ray and Nancy, we saw the heartache as they tried to find another £2 million in the US and in the UK, meeting millionaires and billionaires, applying to foundations, going through endless disappointments. Finally, as the building work on the new complex almost stopped through lack of finance, we decided to step in and give NGM everything they needed to complete the project.

We have been blessed a hundred times over by the work of NGM – all our family have been touched – but above all we have witnessed the power and the light of this vision in the lives of so many young singers, dancers, musicians, sound engineers, disc jockeys, choreographers, and composers. We have also seen the impact of NGM on audiences throughout Britain.

In 2005, Ray devised a show that expressed so much of the love, joy, beauty, and courage of the NGM family in the form of a spectacular biblical musical called *Luv Esther*.

Esther, of course, is the Jewish girl who is chosen to be the bride of the great and fearful King Xerxes, ruler of the greatest empire in the world at the time. Esther's great beauty and strong character, guided by her uncle, Mordecai, becomes the key to the salvation of her people, who are threatened with genocide.

It is one of the great biblical stories and is full of powerful contemporary themes. Beauty and sensuality become a fragrant offering to God, powerful weapons for righteousness and justice. This is a book that celebrates the human body (rather than repressing sexuality, as is sadly the case in many Christian traditions) and also explores the human soul, as Esther struggles with a life-and-death challenge to be truly courageous, to stand against evil at all costs. It was the perfect story for NGM's rich expression of song and dance, music, and artistic exploration.

When Ray first mentioned the concept for this show, I was very excited. We both felt that the world needed a generation of "Esthers" (male and female) who would use their God-given gifts to make a difference. Here was a chance to create a show that was full of beauty, powerful music, high drama – which could offer people a challenge to stand up and be counted and to reckon with the words of Mordecai: "Who knows – you may have come to the kingdom for such a time as this." We decided to link the show to raising money for Sparrow Rainbow Village in South Africa and to encourage our young British audience to think of all the issues around them and in the world beyond.

It was a first for the Lancaster Foundation, but we decided to back a touring stage musical. Ray approached the playwright and director Murray Watts, one of the founding directors of Riding Lights Theatre Company in York, and a well-known writer for radio, TV, and film. Murray and Ray had met a few times in the 1980s, but this was the beginning of a very fruitful collaboration and friendship. Riding Lights are well known for dramatizing the Bible, often using laughter and comedy, and Murray was able to bring many touches of humour and entertainment to the show. He had also written the film *The Miracle Maker* (2000) and knew a lot about large-scale biblical productions in musical theatre. Together, Ray (Writer/Producer), Murray (Writer/Director) and an outstanding team of musicians, dancers, and singers, along with the brilliant West End stage designer Sean Cavanagh, created a glorious spectacle that was truly inspiring. Everywhere the show went, people loved it and were stunned by the combination of great beauty and spirituality: suddenly, it seemed, the hearts of men, women, and children in the audience were catching fire as the great challenge appeared in flaming letters across the darkened stage: "Who knows whether you have come to the kingdom for such a time as this?" (Esther 4:14, NKJV).

I am proud to say that my own children have been prepared to "stand up and be counted" as Christians – and as young people called to make a difference in the world. We hear a lot about "family trees" and genealogy these days, but nothing is more important than the spiritual family tree, which grows and spreads its branches as faith and love are passed down the generations. This is the reason I began writing this book, for the benefit of my grandchildren – but now, I hope, it is for many others who will see themselves as like Esther, realizing that anyone can be "in the right place at the right time". God calls us all to make a difference, however nervous we may be, or however humble our circumstances. I am living proof of this, but it is not about setting up charities; it is simply about following in the footsteps of Christ Himself.

About fifteen years ago, my daughter Julie was an "Esther" for a while as she went out to help with a medical mission in Tanzania. Julie is a trained nurse and is very dedicated to her profession. Her warm and loveable character, full of outrageous humour (like her father), makes her a wonderful carer, bringing joy wherever she goes. But no one, least of all Julie, could have imagined the strange set of circumstances that would turn this Tanzanian medical trip into a major project of social action in inner-city Manchester. The fact is, Julie was in the right place at the right time – and another way of saying this is: God's timing is perfect.

There were two other volunteers on the project, called Simon and Julia Hawthorne. Julie was telling Simon a bit about the work of the Lancaster Foundation in Africa and for NGM when he said, "My brother's an amazing character. He's in a band called The Worldwide Message Tribe and they're going into schools and halls in some of the toughest areas of Manchester. He's passionate about bringing hope and light to people who are living on the edge in the UK. Maybe your parents should meet him…"

Within a few weeks, Julie had set up a meal for six of us: Andy and Michelle Hawthorne, John and me, and Julie and her husband, Phil. I must say, I was very taken with Andy's immense energy, his wacky, off-the-wall personality, and his huge vision for young people. He told us how he had been running a hat business in Manchester, which had suffered some serious break-ins. It soon became clear that the guilty parties were local lads who had been working for him. Instead of being angered and embittered by this, Andy was determined to do something for these "scallies"… He turned a bad situation into a project that was dedicated to youth ministry in the inner city.

We went to see him perform in The Worldwide Message Tribe. They did a song that was called "Jumping in the House of God" – literally, in their case. It was wild, enthusiastic, crazy, funny – without any of the grace and artistry of NGM, but with incredible raw passion. Andy, I have to say, would not have made a career as a dancer, but he had plenty of charisma and power to make up for any technical deficiencies.

Something about this mad band of young performers seized the imagination of many people, and the great thing was that the "tribe" were about touching hearts and changing lives, not just through their performances but in practical and down-to-earth projects.

Before long, John and I found ourselves working alongside volunteers on the most deprived council estates in Manchester. We were handing out tools and paints for the renovation of a local community centre; we were helping in a huge marquee where they had bands, comic sketches, dancers, disc jockeys… a temporary skate park was set up… the whole thing was like a jamboree, with the atmosphere of a fairground: celebration, love, the gospel in action – and it was all free.

One young lad said, "I can't believe this – why do you want to do all this for nowt?"

We were soon offering significant financial support to the amazing work of what became known as The Message Trust. Like the best visionaries, Andy was always bursting with new ideas – and one of his brightest was to buy a couple of buses and turn them into mobile high-tech youth centres with PlayStations® and computer games, activities, and coffee bars.

John was so taken with this scheme that he stood up at a fundraising dinner for it and announced: "I'm in big trouble. I've forgotten Rose's birthday present, so I'm going to buy her a bus – and give it to you, Andy!"

So I had a bus named after me, which was a really great birthday present – a bus that would bless thousands of young people. I have travelled to many interesting places and I can look at some great monument like the Colosseum in Rome and think, "Oh, that's very nice", but my experiences with The Message Trust in Manchester have given me something very different. When I see those "scallies" and look into their eyes – and see the excitement – I know that this is the place I want to be.

I am truly excited when I see love in action and dedicated people making a huge difference, whether in Africa or Manchester. Andy's Eden Project has seen as many as seventy-five families move from wealthy and suburban areas to live on challenging council estates and be a "faithful presence", bringing practical Christian love and inspiration, lived out

Rosemary's bus in Manchester.

day by day in a spirit of joyful social action, hospitality, and compassion. When I see the people influenced by this, young and old – people who have experienced tremendous hardship in their lives – when I see joy and gratitude in their faces – it just breaks my heart, but in the most beautiful way, if that is not too much of a contradiction.

It makes me think of the woman with the alabaster jar in the gospel story. She breaks it open and pours the incredibly expensive perfume over the feet of Jesus. It says that the whole house "was filled with the fragrance" – and no doubt it flowed out of the windows, and down the street to rich and poor alike: Pharisees, beggars, prostitutes, merchants, good and bad; everyone who happened to be passing… For the gospel is really uncontrollable, and the grace of God is for everyone. This is why I love the wild generosity of a spirit like Andy Hawthorne's and why it is so important for us to support people like him.

A few years ago, Andy wrote about his project and the support received from the Lancaster Foundation, so I will let him summarize what has been achieved in his own words:

I am the Founder and Chief Executive of The Message Trust, a charity focused on reaching the hardest-to-reach young people, initially in Greater Manchester, but now all across the UK in schools, communities, and Young Offenders Institutions.

Over the last nineteen years we have achieved growth from one employee to around eighty paid staff plus hundreds of volunteers, many of whom live long-term on the nation's toughest estates.

The trust has benefited immeasurably, not just from the financial giving of the Lancasters, but from their hands-on commitment. I well remember them working alongside many hundreds of young people for a whole week to renovate gardens, remove hundreds of tons of rubbish, and paint many old people's homes, all with involvement from Greater Manchester Police. The police, after this project, identified a 45 per cent reduction in crime.

Our work touches the lives of around 100,000 young people each year, many of them from the most vulnerable backgrounds. We have seen around 300 people move to live on Manchester's most deprived estates and recent research has shown that our programmes reduce prisoner reoffending rates within two years from 62 per cent to only 11 per cent. Again, much of this is as a result of the Lancaster Foundation's hands-on support.

Throughout his business career, John was a visionary pioneer able to see opportunities before others. He has maintained this approach in his charitable giving.

As a trust, we have recently embarked upon our most ambitious project to date – an initiative to provide jobs and mentoring for ex-offenders and other workless young people. I went to share the vision with John and Rose over lunch two weeks ago and they were both visibly moved by the stories of young people with no hope or opportunities and immediately made a pledge of £500,000 on top of their ongoing support for our prisons work, community buses, and school for excluded children.

So often, the first people who supported a new programme we wanted to embark upon were John and Rose Lancaster.

The danger of quoting such heartfelt appreciation is that it looks as if we are "blowing our own trumpet" – but that is not my intention. I want to paint a picture of what has been achieved through grace, through a series of miracles, which began when John and I discovered the love and forgiveness of Christ, when we were truly converted from a selfish way of life to a gradual and powerful understanding that our lives were now "no longer our own" but, as the Bible says, we had been "bought with a price". We began a new journey of following Christ day by day and learning, in our own small way, to be like Esther. The true meaning of our lives was to be found in blessing others. There are many very clever, capable, and extremely hard-working people, including inventors and entrepreneurs, who never make a fortune and never have the opportunity to use it in this way. But the grace of God created a financial miracle for us. We have a clear responsibility to use our money, our time, and our remaining energy wisely. But I can honestly say that it is the most joyful responsibility, the most exciting task we have ever had – and far more rewarding and thrilling than the passing euphoria of business success.

A miracle of grace also brought Ray and Nancy Goudie into our lives… and, many years later, Andy and Michelle Hawthorne. We are the ones who have been blessed.

CHAPTER FOURTEEN

Open Arms International

One of the greatest gifts in life is true friendship. I have learned that friendships, old and new, can help to change the world. It's one thing to have projects and schemes and great plans to make a difference, to relieve poverty and hardship, to transform society, but it's another to make the relationships that lie at the heart of any worthwhile enterprise. Love and friendship give deep roots to a vision.

Looking back, I realize that special friendships have often been the most precious and influential forces in everything the Foundation has achieved. Our story is not about business success but about relationships. Corinne McClintock, Ray and Nancy Goudie, Andy and Michelle Hawthorne… without that true connection, without the spark of friendship setting fire to our hearts, very little would have happened.

We first met David and Rachel Gallagher through Andy Hawthorne (friends create friends!). They were from Portland, USA, and had travelled to Manchester to work with the evangelist Luis Palau on a mission. I remember that they were great fun to be with and, between the two of them, they had a fascinating background. David had studied theology and business, and Rachel was a paediatric nurse who was very passionate about her calling and had even worked alongside Mother Teresa in Calcutta.

Our meeting was brief and it could have been just another very pleasant but passing acquaintance. We flew off to our holiday home in Switzerland but, while we were there, David happened to ring John.

"I'm in Switzerland right now," said John.

"Oh, really? We're about to visit some friends in Switzerland."

"Where are you staying?"

"In a place called Villars."

"Villars! That's just where we are! You'll have to come round for dinner."

David later wrote, "That dinner would change our lives for ever." It was the beginning of our close friendship with David and Rachel but it was also a time when David and Rachel formed a growing bond with two of our oldest and greatest friends, Bob and Liz Edwards.

Soon after this, John was planning a crazy sixtieth birthday bash at Luttrellstown Castle outside Dublin in Ireland. This was for just twelve or so very special couples. Naturally, Bob and Liz were on the list of invitees, but because of Liz's recent eye surgery they were unable to go.

This was very disappointing for them, but John and I decided to ask them to nominate a couple to attend in their place. We have always loved surprising people with

good news, and this was a fun moment, because David and Rachel were so shocked to be included in this inner circle of love and celebration. I'll let David put it in his own words:

Sometime in early October 2003 we were gobsmacked to receive an incredible invitation by post to John's sixtieth birthday party. Only weeks later, we flew out with a group of people who were complete strangers to us. We both felt a bit awkward but also quite humbled to be included in this group of people, most of whom knew each other very well. To make matters either better or worse, we were also the only Americans.

John and Rosemary, hardly knowing Rachel and me at all, treated us as though we were the honoured guests that weekend. Of all the rooms in the castle, we were given one of the only suites to stay in. On the big medieval banquet night when we really celebrated John's birthday, he said to us, "Tonight you're going to sit where you belong – at the head of the table, with Rose and me." We pinched ourselves. We couldn't understand or comprehend this favour to us…

I should add that this was, in fact, a very surreal context for the beginning of a great friendship and a joint missionary enterprise. John was wearing a doublet and hose and a floppy hat, and I was dressed up like Guinevere in a pointed hat and veil. David and Rachel and all the other guests were in equally outlandish medieval costumes. To be honest, I think John should really have been dressed as the court jester, because he was fooling around all evening. I am pleased that David and Rachel came away with such a good impression, but I'm not quite sure how this was possible. Snippets of American films were being imitated at one point and I think I heard someone say to David, "Hey pardner,

Rosemary and John at his 60th birthday
celebration at Luttrellstown castle.

I'm gonna bust your ass!" David was being initiated into
Lancaster family humour and he passed the test with flying
colours. The Gallaghers greatly added to the laughter and
celebration of that occasion, which ended with a ceilidh
band and dancing into the small hours.

It's a pity that words like "missionary" and "relief workers"
do not often appear in the same sentence as "dancing" and

"celebration", but it is important to remember that the same Jesus who healed people and fed the five thousand turned 120 gallons of water into wine at a wedding feast and was criticized by religious leaders for spending too much time at parties! It's true of course that He was a "man of sorrows" who bore the sins and sufferings of the whole world, but He also knew a great deal about joy and celebration.

David and Rachel were natural friends for us, because they knew how to live life to the full – and they were also passionately serious about what God had called them to do. A few weeks after the birthday party in Ireland, they came to dinner again. We asked them what they were going to do when Mission 2000 was over. It turned out that David was retiring from the Luis Palau organization and Rachel was going back to paediatric nursing.

"Is that what you really want to do?" I asked them.

They then poured out their hearts about the suffering of children in the developing world. They wanted nothing more than to meet those desperate needs, whether in Africa or India or elsewhere. They had run medical clinics and relief projects on previous trips abroad and they knew that this was the deepest calling of their lives.

John surprised them once again, this time with an invitation to follow their dream.

"If that's what you want to do, go for it. We'll support you."

Once again, David and Rachel were "gobsmacked".

I nodded at them and smiled.

"Really?"

"Yes, we'd like to launch you."

This was how Open Arms International was born. For some years, Open Arms was working in a variety of countries before David and Rachel established the Open Arms Village in a town called Mlango, just outside the city of Eldoret in Kenya. This is a truly visionary project, but, even before the village came into being, I was privileged to watch David and Rachel at work in a very challenging context.

David and Rachel Gallagher with their children, Belle and Diana.

On 26 December 2004, deep under the Indian Ocean, tectonic plates collided, causing a massive earthquake and tsunami. It was an unforgettable Boxing Day tragedy. While many British families, including our own, were relaxing after the feasting and celebration of Christmas Day, we were confronted with news reports of one of the most shocking natural disasters in the history of the world. Aceh in Indonesia was the hardest hit, followed by Sri Lanka, India, and Thailand. The epicentre was on the west coast of Sumatra, Indonesia. No one who saw them will forget the images of a great wall of water, broken buildings, rubbish, trees, cars, and helpless people sweeping inland, destroying everything in its wake. It was a truly apocalyptic scene and it must have seemed like the end of the world to so many. Some 230,000 people lost their lives in fourteen countries, with 677,599 people displaced. Nations across the world provided £9 billion in humanitarian aid.

But unfortunately the Dalits in India received no help or financial support. The reason for this is that the Dalits are the lowest caste in India, often referred to as "untouchables" – and these are the people David and Rachel wanted to help.

In 2005, Open Arms organized humanitarian aid and medical clinics in Nellore in the province of Andhra Pradesh, south-eastern India. David and Rachel created a team of volunteers, consisting of ten Americans, plus myself and friends Jilly Farthing, Gill Riley, and Tim Funnel, and my son Steven.

We flew into Chennai and on arrival we were met by a young Indian pastor called Rufus. He had a good sense of humour and a great laugh – and I loved him immediately. His parents had founded an orphanage. There were so many poor families who couldn't afford to keep all their children, and many little ones were sent out onto the streets to beg, leaving them very vulnerable and in danger of abuse. The orphanage was a haven of safety and hope for so many and this was to be our home for the next two weeks.

I was looking forward to meeting all the children but Rufus smiled and explained, "We still have five hours' travel, I'm afraid." There were gentle sighs and muffled groans as we tried to adjust to the overwhelming heat and humidity. The journey was a nightmare. The roads were in total darkness, with massive trucks travelling at speed and honking their horns at vehicles that loomed out of the blackness with no headlights! Two and a half hours later, our bus came to a halt. Rufus stood up and, with a completely straight face, said: "Would anyone like the pissy?"

We fell about laughing. Steven was almost uncontrollable and kept repeating the phrase…

Rufus was laughing too but he explained that this was a perfectly normal and acceptable term. I have often considered saying this, with a deadpan expression, to polite English guests at our home in Clitheroe: "Would anyone like the pissy?", but so far I have resisted the temptation.

There are many stories I could tell you but one I remember vividly was the trip to an island medical clinic. Early one morning, our team climbed into a large canoe type of boat, in which we were packed like sardines. It was already very hot and the boat trip was only part of the journey. We were soon trekking quite a distance to a village where a marquee had been erected for the clinic. The temperature was now 35°C and there was 90 per cent humidity. It seemed the whole island had turned up. Gill and I were in charge of weighing babies and giving them worm medication and drops of vitamin A. Rachel worked tirelessly with the medical team, treating the more serious cases. Steve and Tim were on crowd control, because tempers got frayed as anxious people waited in the intense heat.

The island was devoid of sanitation and toilets, and people just had to find a rock or a bush to squat behind. Throughout the day, I drank two litres of water but not once did I need the loo – which was a small but genuine miracle as far as I was concerned. My Indian cotton Punjabi suit was a real blessing, consisting of a long tunic with side slits and oversized trousers – perfect modesty cover when needs arise. I have an amusing memory of ten ladies wearing Punjabis, crouching in line by the side of a sandy road, the only traffic being a man pedalling a bike piled high with branches of wood and an ox pulling a heavy cart. Luckily, the man couldn't see anything because of the wood, and the ox was looking tactfully in the opposite direction.

At the end of the day, exhausted, we made our way to the boat. Unfortunately, halfway across the lake the engine failed, just as the last rays of the sun disappeared. With hardly any wind, the sail was hopeless. We were stuck. There was nothing for it: we needed a volunteer to swim for help, and we all voted for Mr Muscle Man Steven. I was rather worried about what might be lurking in the depths, however: *Jaws III* and *Indian Swamp Monster IV* were already playing in my mind. Steven jumped in like a hero and everyone cheered. His head soon came above water and, I am glad to say, it was still attached to his body. In fact, his head, chest, and waist emerged in quick succession and he was soon standing on his feet, laughing.

"The water's shallow! We can push the boat to the mainland!" So Steven and an Indian volunteer led us to the shore, guided only by a few lights now twinkling in the gathering darkness.

Our medical clinics, in various villages, assessed and treated almost 3,000 people in the space of eight days. We treated many tropical skin conditions such as scabies and boils, and we worked with a number of Indian doctors, dressing wounds and attending to more serious cases.

Later, Rachel wrote an article about this experience, which she headed with a quote from the Bible: "For I am the Lord, who heals you" (Exodus 15:26, NIV). There is no separation in the Christian life between praying for healing and working for healing. Humanitarian aid and medical care can be true expressions of God's love – and that's how we all felt in this land that had been so deeply affected by the tsunami, alongside all its other problems of poverty and deprivation. We felt the privilege of quietly bringing God's love and healing in whatever way we could. I'll let Rachel continue the next part of this story in her own words:

On Monday 20 June 2005, we had already been hard at work for several hours in our medical clinic in a small coastal village about two hours from the city of Nellore. Sometime around 2 p.m., finally at the front of the line of people to be examined, stood two boys, eleven and twelve, whose obvious problem was each one's right foot – wrapped in dirty, soiled rags. Their faces and their feet – yes, their feet – will forever be etched in our minds.

When I unwrapped the first boy's foot, I winced at the sight and the smell: gangrene had already begun its ugly work in his toes. The other boy's foot injury was equally serious. I knew that, without immediate medical attention and most likely surgery, neither boys had long to live, as infection was already ravaging their feet.

Penchalia and Srinivasulu had been electrocuted at the same time as they stood in the back of a truck that carried the statue of a Hindu god. They were participating in a religious festival when an overhead power line snapped and came down on the truck in which they were riding. The electricity coursed through their little bodies, looking for a means of escape. It finally chose to exit through their feet.

The two fathers, nervous and scared, brought their boys to Nellore and we took them to the hospital. We also made every effort to care for the fathers and their sons by feeding them and making them comfortable and assuring them that the costs of the boys' treatment would be taken care of. One father was afraid that he would have to sell the family plot of ground that he farmed for the family's food in order to pay for his son's injuries.

It was amazing that amputation, which had seemed almost inevitable, was not necessary, and the boys made a recovery owing to excellent treatment.

After only twenty-four hours of being with us in the city, one father said, 'I know now that God has been watching out for us and for our sons. We didn't need to be afraid. From this day I am giving my life to the Lord Jesus Christ and will be following Him. I will never turn back.' He left that afternoon to return to his village and give a report on how the boys were being taken care of and how God had so faithfully met them and provided for them.

Another thing that makes this story interesting is that we weren't even supposed to be in that particular village at that time. An unforeseen, last-minute schedule change sent us to the boys' village that day.

During this time, Open Arms also provided the resources for three different villages to have a total of 100 huts built. These brick huts replaced the very small thatched ones that are so easily destroyed in severe tropical weather. The huts were built on concrete foundations and not on the sand that the thatched huts were built on. All this brought back to me memories of Sunday school and the story of the wise and foolish men, one who built his house upon the rock and the other who built his house upon the sand. I realized that many people in the West, including John and myself before we came to faith in God, are living in houses built on the sand. We may not face actual tsunamis in Britain, but broken marriages, personal crises, and bereavement, not to mention the global realities of financial collapse, terrorist threats, and war, can sometimes sweep all our securities away. The greatest danger in a country that is materially well-off is a kind of complacency: "Things will always be this way." Travelling to India reminded me of the simplest and most important realities of life.

One day, we visited a village where the people relied on the sea for their livelihood. The fishermen took us to the beach, which had been hit by devastating waves. They explained that the tsunami had destroyed their fish bed. It was so beautiful that morning, with the gentle waves breaking on the white sand, that it was hard to imagine the terror of that fateful day.

But even in the midst of sorrowful memories and hardship, there was great rejoicing. An elder told us that they would never again have to walk two miles a day for fresh water. They now had a tap in the village, with water piped from a natural source. We had the privilege of watching the oldest resident as he had the honour of turning the tap on. His expression was priceless – a wrinkled face of pure ecstasy – as the water began to spill from the tap. I thought, "Wow… this water is liquid gold to these people!" The old man danced; he cried; the children screamed with delight. I resolved never to take water flowing from a tap for granted, ever again.

In the midst of all the shouting and dancing and excitement, Pastor Rufus raised his hand. He settled the children down and told them a wonderful story from the Bible. This time it was about a woman drawing water from a well. To many people, she was an outcast, an untouchable, forced to draw water alone in the middle of the day when the sun was at its hottest. But Jesus had time for her and He showed His love by sitting down beside her. As they drank water together, He told her about a gift that He could give anyone who believed in Him – "living water", a well deep inside, which bubbled up and filled a person with wonderful joy and power. Everyone listened in rapt attention, the water dripping from the tap like soft music in the background.

It is not until you travel to hot countries where water is scarce and very precious that it is possible to understand the many references to wells, rivers, and streams of water in the Bible:

The Lord is my shepherd;
I shall not want.
He makes me to lie down in green pastures;
He leads me beside still waters.
He restores my soul…

Psalm 23 (NKJV)

When I got back to the orphanage, high-flying spiritual thoughts about water soon came down to earth with a comical crash. We had had problems with the water pressure for showering and all I had managed to do was fill a bucket to use later. Feeling grubby and smelly, I turned on the shower and once again there wasn't a single drip, but I thought, "Thank goodness for the bucket!" I washed myself and my hair as best I could, and wrapped myself in a towel, feeling clean at last. Jilly popped her head round the door.

"How's it going?"

"I feel great – I've just washed my hair from the bucket!"

"What? You just washed your hair with the *bucket water*?"

The look of guilt on Jilly's face gave everything away… as did the dripping knickers and socks on the towel rail!

The trip to India, and a number of other clinics and places abroad, were all stages on the journey towards the Open

Arms Village in Mlango, outside Eldoret in Kenya.

After much travelling, David and Rachel believed that God was calling them to settle in one place and concentrate their work there. It was the place they would come to call home.

The fifty-two acres that make up the Open Arms Village were purchased in late 2007 and construction officially began in the spring of 2009. Since that time, nine children's homes, a baby home, three River View guest lodges, eight one-room guest huts, a bakery, five school buildings, and a medical unit have been built. There is a dairy and poultry compound and a massive garden as part of a drive towards self-sufficiency and sustainability. This is now the beating heart of the ministry of David and Rachel Gallagher – and John and I are thrilled to have played a part in it.

Rosemary and Linda on their first visit to the Open Arms Village.

We decided to dedicate the land to Erin Lily Grace, first child of Steven and Anna, born on 13 July 2004. Erin is tender-hearted and sweet; she dances and plays the flute and she loves every creature on earth – yes, even spiders – so an African dedication is very suitable for her! I hope that her tenderness and creativity will be among the qualities that mark the children blessed by the Open Arms Village. A gentle spirit is a truly precious gift.

Before long, we were able to dedicate two of the new children's homes to our grandchildren Levi Bono, son of Julie and Phil, and Gracie Leigh, daughter of Steven and Anna.

Levi was born on 5 March 2006 and has always been a bundle of fun, enjoying life and playing football (he's a great goalkeeper!), and he has grown up with wonderful good humour and a calm and placid temperament. I have no doubt that he would be quite at home playing with the children at Open Arms and delighting in their company. His children's home has the inscription: "Blessed are the peacemakers, for they will be called sons of God" (Matthew 5:9, NKJV).

As for Gracie, his cousin, born a few months later on 14 September 2006, she has a very giving nature; she is so perceptive, thoughtful, and honest in her responses… she has lots of stage presence and determination – I think she will win many friends in the future. It is very special to me to name a children's home at Open Arms after her, because she is truly someone who opens her arms to others. Her home has the inscription, "Blessed are the pure in heart, for they shall see God" (Matthew 5:8).

The Open Arms family in 2015.

Kenya alone has more than 2.3 million orphans, and 1.2 million of them are directly affected by HIV/AIDS. Eldoret, a city of 650,000 people, has 3,000 children living on its streets. The Open Arms Village has been created to provide a place for some of these children to grow up in a safe and loving family environment, receive an education, and be equipped with life and vocational skills that will prepare them to be future leaders of the country. At the time of writing, Open Arms is caring for more than 100 children. The Open Arms Academy has approximately 165 children enrolled in the school and 100 of these are from the community surrounding the village.

It's now many years since John and I asked David and Rachel what they *really* wanted to do with their lives and offered to launch their project with them. They have been faithful to their vision.

But the best kind of charity and philanthropy is always a two-way process – a "double blessing", if you like. I feel that my own life has been transformed by many of the projects we have supported, and Open Arms has truly helped me to open my arms – and my heart – wider than ever before.

I've come to understand that God sometimes uses sensitive personalities (people like me who are naturally prone to anxiety and troubled emotions, as well as to great enthusiasm and excitement!) as his special ambassadors. He forms and shapes our characters, often through hardship, so we can discover true empathy – so we can begin to feel what God feels for other people in need. It's easy to be caught up in our own thoughts, but I am convinced that God wants us to be full of His thoughts and His emotions. Our default position as sensitive people is frequently self-obsession – and that is the opposite of our true destiny.

We have been created in the image of God and we are meant to have sensitive antennae to His Holy Spirit. Sometimes this means following a gut feeling, a deep-down conviction that can lead to immediate action.

My next adventure was all to do with watching a TV documentary and it took me back to Kenya, only this time right onto the rubbish heaps of Eldoret, where street children were living in desperate conditions.

CHAPTER FIFTEEN

The Solomon Project

Ross Kemp is a well-known TV actor, with a very compassionate heart. He has visited many dangerous locations in the world but nothing has affected him as deeply as the stinking rubbish heaps of Eldoret, home to thousands of street children.

The year was 2008 and there had been an outbreak of savage violence on the streets of Kenya, following charges of corruption and vote-rigging in the General Election.

A young boy called Danson, when we first met him in Eldoret.

The number of homeless and frightened children in Eldoret trebled, from 1,000 to 3,000. Ross Kemp visited the infamous rubbish dumps to make a documentary for Sky One, with the charity Save the Children.

Picture the scene…

Filthy children scavenging and fighting for scraps of rotten food.

Mothers and toddlers with glue bottles stuck to their front teeth.

Gang violence and brutalization by the police.

Young girls, victims of rape, giving birth in horrific squalor.

Children everywhere, hungry, thirsty, afraid, sheltering under plastic sheets, trying to escape from their misery by sniffing glue or drinking lethal home brews of alcohol.

Fear, hatred, crime, utter desperation.

Boys and girls being abused.

This is surely a picture of hell on earth… and it was a hell I came to visit because of Ross Kemp's haunting film.

This is what he said about his overwhelming experience: "That sight will stay in my mind for the rest of my life… it shocked me to the core." Ross soon realized that the whole seething community on those sprawling rubbish tips was addicted to glue. "When a woman drops her child on its head and picks it up and puts a glue bottle in its mouth, those are the things that stay with you; to see that loss, that desperation."

I sat there, tears streaming down my face, watching those

harrowing scenes unfold, the eyes of children who had lost all hope, the faces of people who stared sightlessly out of their hovels in the trash, as if their humanity was being snuffed out by a terrible darkness.

I was terribly shaken by this and I could not settle for hours after seeing the film.

I went to bed praying, "God, what can we do to help?"

After a fitful sleep, I woke up in the middle of the night to hear a voice. It spoke softly out of the darkness of my bedroom – and it was not in my imagination.

"Rose, go to Eldoret."

This is the only time something as direct as this has ever happened to me. I certainly have deep feelings, as you already know! I have strong convictions, I sometimes have ideas and plans, and I have often listened and responded to calls for help from other people. I did once hear mysterious and beautiful singing in Norway, almost like a dream. But this experience was somehow very different. A voice, very clear, spoke to me:

"Rose, go to Eldoret."

I can't explain why this happened to me on this particular occasion, and I don't think that I or any other Christian should really seek out this kind of special experience, because we have been given minds and hearts to respond to God and His world. We can choose to act out of compassion or even out of sheer common sense. We can act in a natural way without needing anything supernatural. And there is a danger too, in cases of dramatic spiritual stories, of people saying, "Well, why hasn't this happened to *me?*"

This is why I have hesitated to share this moment, even with my closest family. But it is an important part of my own story.

You can read of such things in the Bible, especially in the story of Samuel, who was only a small boy. He was lying down to sleep one night in the Temple where he lived and was serving the High Priest, Eli, and he heard a voice calling his name: "Samuel, Samuel." Three times the boy went to Eli and said, "Here I am; you called me," and Eli replied, "I did not call; go back and lie down." But eventually Eli realized what was happening and said to Samuel, "If the voice calls again, say, 'Speak, Lord, for your servant is listening'" (1 Samuel 3:2–10). And so began Samuel's life as a prophet, listening to God and obeying His word.

Well, I am no prophet and I am certainly not like Samuel – except in one respect. I believe that when the voice of God comes, whether it is through a set of circumstances, through our conscience being challenged, through a reading of Scripture, through a sermon, through a friend, through watching a film, through a dream, through anything that calls our heart to action – even through something as rare as an actual voice or a vision – we should say, like Samuel, "Speak, Lord, for your servant is listening."

I am seventy years old now (it's hard to keep this a secret when I've had two major birthday celebrations). This is the full biblical span for a human life, yet I hope to live a lot longer to watch my grandchildren grow up and to celebrate their lives and to keep on loving them and rooting for them in every way. But I hope you'll agree that, at this special age, I have perhaps earned the right to share with you the most precious advice. When God speaks, in whatever way, listen very carefully and obey.

Within a week, I was on my way to Eldoret. My companion was a very dear friend, Linda, wife of Chris Richardson, who is the development director of the Lancaster Foundation. Linda had already been out to Kenya on a trip to the Open Arms Village. Like me, she had been overwhelmed by the Ross Kemp documentary.

"I watched the film with our son, Philip," she said later. "I watched in disbelief. The more I watched, the more tears flowed at the sad, vague, helpless, lost faces. There I was in my comfortable home with my son, whom I loved to bits, and I looked at these children – nowhere to go, and no one to love them and take care of them. How could this happen? All this was happening in Eldoret, where I had been with the Open Arms team only eighteen months before. I felt disturbed and the images preyed on my mind. What could be done to help? When Rose asked me to go with her, I knew this would take me way beyond my comfort zone… however, I felt that God had prepared me for this and I was sure He would look after us."

On arrival, I called Charlotte from the Save the Children Rapid Response Team (who had been involved in the documentary) and she gave us a thorough briefing for our trip. She also linked us with three young men who had once been on the streets and were now trying to help others. They became our willing guides to the huge dump known locally as "The Barracks".

As we approached the dump, boys surrounded our vehicle. We felt threatened. It was black and dirty and we were faced with these boys with hoods and glue bottles hanging from their mouths. My heart was racing. Linda and I held hands. For one fleeting moment I wondered if I had done the right thing. I was grateful for the reassuring presence of our guides.

But soon, "peace like a river" began to flow around me. I knew that I was following my heart and that "perfect love casts out fear". In minutes, inquisitive children emerged from the dump, acknowledging the team and smiling at the strange visitors from far-off Clitheroe.

I thought, "England is as remote to these children as Eldoret is to us." And even while witnessing the deprivation and tragedy all around, I thought of young people on the streets of Manchester, Birmingham, and London – drug addicts, homeless people, and victims of sex trafficking and abuse. I thought of William Booth's book, *In Darkest England*. But here we were at the extreme edge of human deprivation and suffering, as if all the lost children of the world were concentrated into one terrible, nightmarish existence.

I could see boys lying around, their eyes rolling from too much glue. I saw a desperate makeshift delivery room set up in the trash, where young girls could give birth. I saw people huddling round a small fire, attempting to heat a few scraps of food in a pan. I saw children scavenging for pathetic pieces of plastic, which they could sell for a pittance – only to pay for a dry bread roll or the next sniff of glue. Even while we were staying nearby, visiting "The Barracks" every day, we heard appalling stories of abuse among the children. We met a sixteen-year-old torture victim ourselves.

The tragic truth is that these helpless children were becoming almost indistinguishable from the trash, and the police clearly regarded them as vermin, like rats to be trapped, slaughtered, swept out of sight. What did it matter if another of these infested creatures was lost without trace? Who cared?

God cares, and that is the greatest eternal truth.

"Let the little children come to me," said Jesus, who was angry with His disciples for pushing away mothers with their babies, who were seeking a blessing. "Do not hinder them!" On another occasion, He said of little children, "Their angels in heaven are always beholding the face of my Father in heaven."

We had to keep going and do whatever we could.

On that first day, I saw a small boy whom I noticed particularly. He looked ill and gaunt. I made my way towards him. I smiled and he managed a fleeting smile in return. I offered him one of my bread rolls – a feeble gesture, but he seized it as if it were a bag of gold. He didn't eat it but gripped it firmly in his little fist.

"What's your name?" I asked.

"Danson Macheria."

"How old are you, Danson?"

"Eleven years –"

Just then, a bigger boy pushed him roughly out of the way. Danson stumbled off, covering himself with a piece of dark green plastic.

I felt an overwhelming need to pray. Linda and I knelt down in the dirt and cried out to God to overshadow this place with His presence. For a few moments there was a sense of stillness and calm; a moment of light shining in a very dark world.

As we drove away, tears flowed and I could not speak. My heart screamed out at the injustice. From the rear window, I caught a final glimpse of Danson, his dirty yellow cap disappearing as he ran into the darkness. He was still clutching his bread roll. The haunted expression in his eyes will remain fixed in my memory for ever. I was determined that I had to rescue him from his life of misery. More than anyone, Danson was the inspiration for the Solomon Project, which grew out of this unforgettable trip to the rubbish tips of Eldoret.

There are many reasons why a child can end up trying to survive in the brutal and heartless environment of this hellhole on the margins of urban Kenya. Sheer poverty and deprivation are the most common causes. Parents cannot feed their children, so they are forced to fend for themselves. Broken homes and abusive families cause children to run away, preferring a street gang to a violent father. Alcohol and sexual abuse are dark forces that ravage the lives of many young people. Pregnancy, often involving rape and incest, causes girls to run for their lives – only to land up giving birth in desperate and toxic conditions. Many children are orphans who have lost both parents to HIV/AIDS.

The list is endless and the line of children is endless... I only have to close my eyes now to see thousands of imploring faces, half-buried in that filthy wasteland.

A life on the streets frequently makes matters much worse. It is truly a case of "out of the frying pan and into the fire". Children who leave home without education, without support, without ID cards, are well and truly "off the grid". They have no chance of work. They are nobodies. Street life is not "life" at all – it is a deadly environment where life has no value. It is hardly surprising that children learn to steal for food, snatch and mug as they get older, turn to prostitution, and invariably become drug addicts. Because they are treated like vermin, they begin to act like vermin, living like a sub-species of humanity. They live far below what we would call the "underclass" in the West. It is really hard to plumb the depths of the sadness and inhumanity of this desperate domain – I can only use a biblical phrase, "kingdom of darkness".

What can be done? What do the street children want most of all? We had practical discussions with a number of former street children and they listed their priorities.

First of all, a life without glue – and this means at least three months of safe haven and rehabilitation.

Then, accommodation and emotional and financial support.

The provision of ID cards, with help from social workers to research age verification and financial help for court representation.

Rosemary meets some of those using glue to relieve the pain of hunger.

Education – which means official registration at a school.

Training in skills, so they will eventually be able to earn their own living.

And it was not difficult for me and Linda to add love, faith, and hope – those three great gifts from God mentioned in the Bible. But such precious virtues cannot be separated from food, clothing, welfare, and education… in the Christian life, everything is connected.

What happened with the Solomon Project is a long story, but I will keep this account brief. It began, very humbly, because of this trip.

Linda and I returned to Clitheroe, overflowing with memories and emotions and determination to do something, however small.

One of the greatest initiatives for nineteenth-century "street children" in Britain was undertaken by George

214

Müller, who founded many children's homes. He was a man of extraordinary faith and frequently his resources and his trust in God were stretched to the limit. George Müller wrote this:

> *Faith does not operate in the realm of the possible. There is no glory for God in that which is humanly possible. Faith begins where man's power ends.*

The world is full of apparent "impossibilities", with overwhelming problems of poverty, war, millions of refugees fleeing oppression, one great international crisis after another – and frequently children are the most vulnerable and poignant victims of an adult world that is full of ruthless and selfish people.

I will never forget – no one who saw it will ever forget – the image of that little drowned Syrian boy on a beach in Turkey in 2015. I can only repeat to myself, when faced with such tragedies – and with Danson on the rubbish tip – the words of Mother Teresa. You will remember that she was asked, "How can we change the world?" And she replied, "One person at a time."

When the angel came to Mary, announcing that she would have a child from God who would be the saviour of the world, Mary asked how such a thing could happen, since she was still a virgin. The angel replied gently, "Nothing is impossible with God." People like George Müller and Mother Teresa understood that everything is possible with God and also that the most significant work often begins in very small ways, with one boy, one girl, one man, one woman... The

Virgin Mary is an example of one woman who surrendered herself completely to God. Like Samuel, she said, "Behold, I am the servant of the Lord" (Luke 1:38, ESV).

It was very fitting that, within a few weeks of our return to Britain, I heard of an organization called "Mary's Meals". This Catholic charity, in the spirit of Mary's service to God, had set out to provide millions of school meals for hungry children in the developing world. We met the founder, Magnus MacFarlane-Barrow, a very remarkable man (who in 2015 published a book entitled *The Shed That Fed a Million Children*).

Magnus had already had wide experience of relief work, dating back to the Bosnian War, but the crucial moment came for him when he was in Malawi. He met a starving child whose mother was dying. The little boy told him, "I would like to have enough food to eat and I would like to be able to go to school one day." Mary's Meals was born and it operates out of a humble shed in Magnus's garden in the Highlands of Scotland. The charity buys its supplies in the communities where it serves its meals. Local people supply, grow, and cook the food, a model which is at the heart of the project and, according to Magnus, is the secret of "why it is so robust and works".

We were soon providing daily meals for children in villages and schools around Eldoret. The Solomon Project now feeds 9,500 and our partner, Mary's Meals, has more than doubled that number. As a result of this, school attendance has risen considerably, the prospects of children in the worst slum district of Langas (where many of the street children come from) have improved, truancy has decreased, and educational results have improved.

The Grand in Clitheroe, the theatre and arts project established by the Lancaster Foundation (see next chapter!) has become a partner of the Solomon Project. Linda and I were involved in a very moving evening there, soon after our return from Eldoret, which was really a candlelit vigil for the lost children of the rubbish tips and a heartfelt plea for prayer, love, and financial commitment to make a significant difference. The theatre was full of candles, and photos from that haunting time, and it was a very memorable launch for us – it was as if thousands of children from the streets were gazing at us and saying, "Please help us!"

Steven is the director of The Grand and he went out to Eldoret in November 2013 to see the progress of the project. He said to a local journalist afterwards, "It was my first visit to Eldoret and it was a very profound experience. It brought to life the reality that, in this day and age of technology, we can all embrace our global brothers and sisters. In my visit to Eldoret I saw how the impact of the Solomon Project is very broad. It is certainly helping the lives of individual children, but, much more than that, it is affecting entire communities – especially schools. The Foundation's support, through better nutrition and equipment in kitchens and IT departments, is helping teachers, volunteers, and pupils transform educational standards – and the whole quality of their lives."

The Solomon Project is dedicated to Steven and Anna's third child, Solomon Alfie Emmanuel, who was born on 10 November 2008. Soli, the youngest of my seven grandchildren, is a joy. His winning smile melts your heart; he's an all-round athlete and a fun little man. Football is his first love, and he's always one for a good laugh.

And I cannot look into his face, or the face of any of my grandchildren, without remembering how blessed they are – without feeling such pride and joy – but also without thinking of how many gorgeous children like them are lost out there, in the darkness of our troubled world. But… "One person at a time" and "Nothing is impossible for God".

Oh and I should add that we rescued Danson from his life of misery. He is now eighteen years old and a bright and gifted student who has thrived while living at the Open Arms Village. However, because of problems from his past, and after two deeply emotional experiences while away at secondary school, Danson decided to leave the school (in Kenya, pupils do not attend a local school for secondary education, but have to attend a boarding school).

Danson aged 15 in the Open Arms Village, and a piece of art he completed there.

John and Rosemary with Danson when he was 18.

He is exploring his options for future education and is interested in information technology. Meanwhile, he is working in construction at the Open Arms Village. He has expressed a desire to help other children who find themselves homeless and living on the streets. How wonderful!

When I think about the voice that spoke to me in the night – "Rose, go to Eldoret" – I think it was telling me to find Danson.

A few years ago, I came across an old poem that says it all about the children of Eldoret – and the children of our own "Darkest England" and the Western world too. It's all about the power of music and the great potential of every individual person. My son-in-law, Philip, has been a gifted teacher but now runs his own business repairing and renewing guitars. He is extremely skilful with his hands and has an ambition to become a luthier – a maker of stringed instruments. He has helped to shape the lives of children but now he physically shapes musical instruments... which in turn will shape the lives of others. I find this an inspiring career development! So you can see why the story told in the poem below captured my heart:

The Touch of the Master's Hand

'Twas battered and scarred, and the auctioneer
Thought it scarcely worth his while
To waste much time on the old violin,
But held it up with a smile.
"What am I bidden, good folks," he cried,
"Who'll start the bidding for me?"
"A dollar, a dollar. Then two! Only two?
Two dollars, and who'll make it three?"

"Three dollars, once; three dollars, twice;
Going for three…" But no,
From the room, far back, a grey-haired man
Came forward and picked up the bow;
Then wiping the dust from the old violin,
And tightening the loosened strings,
He played a melody pure and sweet,
As a caroling angel sings.

The music ceased, and the auctioneer,
With a voice that was quiet and low,
Said: "What am I bid for the old violin?"
And he held it up with the bow.
"A thousand dollars, and who'll make it two?
Two thousand! And who'll make it three?

Three thousand, once; three thousand, twice,
And going and gone," said he.

The people cheered, but some of them cried,
"We do not quite understand.
What changed its worth?" Swift came the reply:
"The touch of the master's hand."
And many a man with life out of tune,
And battered and scarred with sin,
Is auctioned cheap to the thoughtless crowd
Much like the old violin.

A "mess of pottage," a glass of wine,
A game – and he travels on.
He is "going" once, and "going" twice,
He's "going" and almost "gone."
But the Master comes, and the foolish crowd
Never can quite understand
The worth of a soul and the change that is wrought
By the touch of the Master's hand.

Myra Brooks Welch, 1921

I first read a version of this in UCB's *Word for Today* magazine, on 15 March 2013. I have often found *Word for Today* inspiring because it is certainly full of belief in the power of God to change anyone, whatever their circumstances. In the case of this lovely old poem, it may not be "great art" as literature but it is good storytelling by any standards. The author says she was inspired by a speaker who preached on the potential of every individual, and then she went home, was "filled with light", and wrote this poem in just thirty minutes. In due course, she sent it to her church magazine and explained that it was a gift from God and she didn't need her name on it!

This is a very different attitude from our own celebrity culture today and much closer to that of the medieval artists who created beautiful stained glass and statues high up in cathedrals – with no signatures, no praise, and no fame. All they wanted was the glory of God.

Although I have been telling my own story in such personal terms, John and I are aware of the risks and the tensions in doing this. We are learning more every day that the only thing that matters, and lasts for ever, is love   and love given for the glory of God.

Steve, Anna and their children Erin, Solomon and Gracie. This project was dedicated to Solomon.

CHAPTER SIXTEEN

Full Circle

There was a famous comedy series on BBC Radio in the 1960s called *The Clitheroe Kid*, starring Jimmy Clitheroe, who took his name from our little Lancashire town, where he was born. The Clitheroe Kid was always getting into terrible scrapes but somehow this mischievous little boy always came out on top.

Like Peter Pan, the Clitheroe Kid never grew up – he was always young, always full of energy, and always getting into trouble. His life was full of ups and downs but the abiding impression was of a life full of adventure, laughter, and joy.

I like to think that John and I have carried on this tradition, which once made our town famous. We're "Clitheroe Kids" – and we haven't grown up, either!

One of my most vivid local memories stays with me… it's sitting with John in the very back row of the "The Grand" Cinema in York Street, Clitheroe, in the early 1960s. Every Saturday, we went to our favourite place, where teenage lovers could sit in the few notorious double seats high up at the back, known as "love seats"… the main idea, as you can imagine, was not to watch the film. Rather stern usherettes

John receives an honorary doctorate from UMIST.

would come and interrupt our intimacy by shining a bright torch in our faces and asking brusquely, "Ice cream, love – tub or choc ice?" We knew the subtext, which was sometimes spelt out literally: "Hey, you, quit that snogging!"

The rest, as they say, is history – one husband, two children and seven grandchildren later – but it is history with a curious twist. The Lancaster Foundation now owns The Grand, and John and I have kept that very same "love seat" as a souvenir!

Here's how it all happened…

We had grown up with The Grand, which had begun life in the heyday of Victorian music halls. It was the home of raucous and hilarious live theatre acts, which, no doubt, were frowned on by the churches. But it was a real centre of community life and celebration, something desperately needed in a Lancashire town where people struggled hard to survive. Eventually, like all the old music halls, The Grand became a cinema and this is how we remembered it. I suppose we all took its familiar and comforting presence for granted… our local cinema, our beloved "fleapit", which was the affectionate slang term of the day. But by the 1980s and 1990s many independent cinemas were falling on hard times and The Grand was no exception. It was in a poor state of repair and the council was forced to take it over. It was run as a cinema for a while, but the council was losing £35,000 a year and closure was imminent.

In the year 2000 we had the idea of renting The Grand for a one-off "Millennium" event, which was particularly aimed at men in Clitheroe. We wanted to share something of the joy and power of the Christian message – in this very special year – with hundreds of men who, as the saying goes, would "never darken the doorstep" of a church. We invited two famous Christian comedians, Tommy Cannon and Bobby Ball, to be our celebrity guests.

Cannon and Ball were simply brilliant. They were hilariously funny, they were honest, they were open about their faith. The Grand was suddenly on fire, not only with the sheer joy of live theatre and comedy, but with the presence of divine love. It was a remarkable evening and our capacity audience of 400 were thrilled and moved.

Later that night I said to John, "We can't let The Grand be turned into a carpet warehouse."

So the idea was formed to save our old theatre, with its long and chequered history, and to make it a centre of life and celebration for the whole community once again. And, like many such dreams, the process took a long while and the pathway was strewn with frustrations, complex negotiations, struggles over planning permission…

The interior of The Grand following the renovation.

With every such enterprise, there are always people who are happy to be "brakes" rather than "accelerators", and around every vision there are often the "nay-sayers" – those who doubt, discourage, list the problems, make sceptical comments. Even as far back as the book of Nehemiah in the Bible, which was written about 400 BC, you can see the forces of discouragement that gathered against Nehemiah's brave project to rebuild the ruined walls of Jerusalem. Sanballat and Tobiah ride past and laugh at the slow progress: "Ha!" they scoff. "A fox could knock down this wall." But Nehemiah prays, "O God, strengthen my hands!" He uses brilliant organization and delegation, and ultimate team-building, to accomplish the work in only fifty days.

John had plenty of experience in project management and successful team-building, and the right kind of psychological make-up to deal with setbacks, so I had no doubt that he would use all this background to save The Grand. But, today, I still regard it as another miracle, an example of God's grace and of His love too, for the people of Clitheroe.

Our vision was not some narrow "Christian" agenda at all, but of a place that would be available to all, where the best music, dance, theatre, and cinema could be enjoyed and, above all, where our young people could be inspired and trained in the arts – and discover new purpose for their lives.

Our son Steven became Executive Director and we are happy to see what he has achieved. In a booklet about The Grand and the experience it now offers, he writes:

The Grand is a state-of-the-art live music and arts concert venue, set in the heart of the Ribble Valley.

We are committed to the cultural, social, spiritual, emotional, educational and personal development needs of young people and the broader community...

We are a community of people who, by the very nature of the work we carry out, are developing, inspiring and unlocking creativity in people through arts, multi-media, music and innovation.

By the beginning of 2013, more than 6,000 young people had accessed and engaged with projects at The Grand, which amounts to a 54% penetration of the local youth population.

We live in an age when schools are under pressure to obtain good results from children in English grammar and maths at very early ages. Many schools are finding it difficult to develop music, theatre, arts, and media in the face of such powerful government pressure to deliver quantifiable results in traditional subjects. But the arts are hugely influential in the world today, so why are we neglecting them?

John and I believe that there are great benefits for Clitheroe in giving young people a multitude of creative opportunities. One of my favourite activities is the "Be My Band" twelve-week course, in which professional musicians teach youngsters how to create and perform in a band. It's right back to Ray Goudie's influence on Steven. Love, friendship, dedicated time, drumming sessions together...

A true Christian vision for society includes every

aspect of life and learning. It is not just about church or "religion"; it is about the spiritual nature of every human being. This was explored powerfully in Ray Goudie's most recent musical, *The Prodigals*, a thrilling production directed by Joe Harmston, which won acclaim and an award at the Edinburgh Festival in 2011. It dramatizes the story of a father's love for his two very different sons and is inspired by the famous parable told by Jesus. The message of the story is quite simply that God is full of overwhelming love for His children, but that such a profound truth has to be experienced emotionally and psychologically; it cannot be taught as some kind of dry sermon. Story, as Jesus knew better than anyone, touches the human soul. It is often through the arts – singing, dancing, acting, painting – that we express our deepest spiritual nature, and it is through the arts that we shape our culture and create what the Chief Rabbi once called "an ecology of hope": in other words, the kind of environment where hope is likely to flourish.

That's how we see the work of The Grand in our own community.

I didn't realize it until recently, but we are continuing in a very honourable tradition here. At the end of the nineteenth century, a remarkable spinster lady called Lilian Baylis took over an old musical hall in Waterloo, London, which was renamed The Old Vic. She was a committed Christian who had a vision to provide good entertainment for ordinary people, an alternative to some of the rough and crude shows on offer in cheap music halls around the country. She began producing Shakespeare, even though she knew nothing about theatre, and was famous for typing letters up in the gallery at The Old Vic whilst watching her actors perform *Hamlet* on the stage… her actors eventually included people such as Laurence Olivier and John Gielgud. From this one woman's vision came Sadler's Wells, the Royal Ballet, the English National Opera, and what we now celebrate as the National Theatre in London. Lilian Baylis would go to All Saints, Margaret Street, off Oxford Street in London, and pray – or usually argue with God – about providing more money for her work!

The Grand is a much humbler enterprise than The Old Vic, but we believe that "small is beautiful" and also that it's "payback" time for us in Clitheroe. We feel that we are called to bring gifts to our local friends, neighbours, and townsfolk. We also believe strongly that the quality of our culture in the north of England matters. We want to make a difference on our own doorstep. At the same time, we are delighted that "The Grand" is twinned with the Solomon Project in Kenya and, because of this and regular fundraising events, Clitheroe people are making a difference to the lives of many children in Africa.

"What goes around, comes around…"

Perhaps our most surprising local project was the creation of a skate park in the Castle Gardens. When this project was suggested to us by our son Steve, who had been talking to an enterprising community youth worker called Jeff Jackson, I couldn't help thinking, "Skate park? In our beautiful Clitheroe gardens? Whatever next? Water Slides for Pensioners on Pendle Hill? Bouncy Castles for Bishops in Blackburn Cathedral?"

But the skate park in our historic gardens has proved to be an inspired idea. There were so many teenagers with little to do in the town, and local people were complaining about skateboarders hurtling towards them on the pavement and across the roads. Steve and Jeff took the view that it is always best to respond positively and creatively to a problem. So we negotiated on the site with the council, the Lancaster Foundation paid for the construction of one of the best skate parks in the country, and it has now become a major recreation centre, with crowds coming every weekend – people often travelling thirty miles or more, just for the fun of it…

The power of fun cannot be underestimated. Sadly, some religious people can lose their sense of fun, like the pious old couple who took the swing out of their budgie's cage every Sunday, in case he enjoyed himself… Weekends are there for recreation and celebration, especially Sundays. It's the first day of the week: new life! Sundays mark the day of the resurrection, which is the heart of the Christian faith. I like the verse in the book of Proverbs that describes wisdom as "ever at play in the world". It is truly wise to have fun.

So I am glad that we have added some fun to the centre of our town. But I was also amazed and touched by a dear friend of mine in our church, Margaret Bleazard, who couldn't go skateboarding but who used the park as an opportunity for prayer. She used to walk through the gardens, watching the children zooming and swerving and twirling in the air, and she would pray for them all. She would ask for God's blessing on their lives. That's what I call a living, practical, and very loving Christian faith. Margaret was a great inspiration to me. She was so innocent, in our modern world, that I remember gales of laughter in one morning service when she was announcing the results of a pancake-making competition. She described a much respected member of the congregation as "the best tosser in this church"!

Margaret prayed all the time for the Lancaster Foundation. Years ago, she was the first person to visit me after my mum died, and I can still feel that hug and see the tears in her eyes… she was a wonderful, compassionate soul. She died some years ago and, along with a multitude of others, I still miss her.

And there's somebody else whom I will miss so much.

Now, even as I am finishing this book, I have just heard that our dear friend Ray Goudie has died. John and I have been heartbroken, along with so many others who have been blessed and encouraged and deeply touched by his wonderful life of faith. We feel so deeply for Nancy and their two sons, Daniel and Aidan. Ray knew where he was going and he believed firmly that God would take him when the time was right – "not a day too soon nor a day too late". He knew that the timing of his departure was not determined by physical illness, but by God.

There are a great many sorrows as well as joys in the pilgrimage of every Christian. And there's a danger in writing a memoir of this kind, which might imply that once I had become a Christian – and once we had made our fortune – life was nothing but a series of "highs", of great spiritual adventures, of wealth, fulfilment, perfect good health…

But this is far from the truth. Only a few years ago, I felt that my faith was tested to the limit. Although it was not the ultimate test of life and death, it felt like a dress rehearsal. The first challenge came on Easter Monday 2008. John and I were finishing a round of golf when he suddenly doubled over in excruciating pain. Having recently returned from Eldoret in Kenya, we thought he had picked up some kind of bug. John was ill for weeks. Procedures and tests revealed that something sinister was going on – a scan showed numerous dark spots on his liver. The prognosis wasn't good. We walked out of the consulting room, arm in arm, trying to hold it together. Words were few and a sense of dread overwhelmed us both. John's consultant came after us, saying, "John, we'll have to arrange to have a biopsy of your liver." I sat in the car as John was making the appointment and my heart was breaking. I desperately needed to hear Julie or Steven's voice, so when I heard Steven say "Hello" on the phone, the floodgates opened…

I blubbered his father's results to him and Steven calmly said, "Just call by on your way home." There, Steve and Anna, Julie and Phil helped us to calm down and encouraged us to pray for strength to deal with whatever lay ahead. Children can be such a blessing and a comfort at times like this. Soon afterwards, our rector, Mark, anointed John with oil and many prayers were said for healing (a Christian tradition since the days of the early church two thousand years ago).

The day of the biopsy arrived and John was mildly sedated as the surgeon inserted a camera into his abdomen. "How does my liver look?" John asked tentatively.

The surgeon replied, "Very healthy; nice colour!" It was almost like the weatherman predicting a fine day at the seaside. A scan confirmed that the dark spots were diminishing. The consultant was a little perplexed, though delighted with the results.

We both felt that God was powerfully at work. But it is important to say that although John's health crisis had passed and he appeared to be all right – even healed! – God would still have been at work even if the news had been bad. The Twenty-Third Psalm, perhaps the best-loved poem in the world, says, "Yea, though I walk through the valley of the shadow of death, I will fear no evil; for thou art with me…" (KJV). God never leaves us, even at the very last. For every one of us is mortal and our lives are ultimately in His hands.

I thought of dear Margaret Bleazard, who had died of cancer but kept on smiling even in her final days because she didn't want people to worry and she wanted to cheer them up. I must admit, I couldn't find Margaret's faith and courage when my own time of testing came.

Two years later, on Easter Monday 2010, John and I were enjoying breakfast and happy to be going out to play golf. This time it was my turn to feel a savage pain in my abdomen. I took two paracetamols and went to lie down, saying, "I'll sleep it off." Five hours later, still in terrible pain and starting to vomit, I agreed to send for the doctor. He diagnosed appendicitis and we were advised to go straight to Accident and Emergency at the Royal Hospital in Blackburn.

This is the point at which I need to say that I really believe in our National Health Service. I am proud of this great achievement, which began at the time when I was born. So many lives have been saved and there has been a huge impact for good on our society. But…

I was about to experience the kind of nightmare that people talk about, when you are in desperate trouble but you get "lost in the system". What happened to me was not good by any standards. It was appalling.

We waited what seemed like an eternity in an overcrowded waiting area. It appeared that the whole of Blackburn had turned up, owing to local surgeries being closed over Easter. Eventually, a doctor examined me. He immediately admitted me to the Triage Unit (where priority for treatment is decided). John found a wheelchair for me but, needless to say, we got lost on the way there. Triage was as chaotic as A&E and staff were running crazily in all directions. By now, I was desperate for some pain relief. A doctor arrived, promising to transfer me on to a ward. He proceeded to take blood from my arm and, to my horror, blood was soon squirting out of my vein onto the floor.

"It's OK; I know what I'm doing," he said, unconvincingly. Soon he started rubbing the blood around on the floor with his foot, mumbling, "The nurses will kill me if they see all this."

I thought, "I don't think we need any more blood around here; one murder is enough." John was beside himself with fury. He thought he was living through a surreal combination of *Carry On Doctor* and *The Return of Dracula*.

Following an unpleasant night, still in Triage, my sense of fair play and willingness to take a back seat was about to be put through the wringer. Typically British, I didn't want to "make a fuss" or, for that matter, jump any queues… But it felt as if the queues were stretching over the horizon.

The days that followed are a jumble of images… Tuesday I am examined by doctor number four: "Not sure what the problem is…" He prescribes intravenous fluid and pain relief.

A senior consultant calls in the afternoon: "Could be an ovarian cyst; not sure. Let's do laparoscopic surgery; prepare this patient for surgery: Nil by Mouth."

A brief moment of relief… I'm on the emergency list; all this will be behind me tomorrow!

Wednesday, still waiting… Staff are struggling to cope, poorly people crowding through the hospital… I know that critically ill people have priority, but I am projectile vomiting, my stomach is swollen, I am in desperate pain. I long for a cup of tea, but it's not allowed: "Nil by Mouth".

Wednesday evening. A nurse arrives smiling and asks, "Do you want the good news or the bad news?" I stare at her in disbelief. "No surgery today, but you are on the list for tomorrow."

I am beginning to feel cold with only a single cotton sheet on my bed. I ask for a blanket but a patient in the next bed to me says, "I've been here since January; there's no spare blankets on this ward. Use your dressing gown." But I've already been sick all over my dressing gown…

Thursday morning. Two porters arrive with a trolley. I start to get out of bed, eager to go to surgery, trying to be helpful. "Can you walk?" one of them asks, in a harsh, accusing tone.

"Well…" I hesitate. "I think I can manage just a little – "

"If you can walk, the most you're getting is a wheelchair. If I can find one!" The porters sweep off with their empty trolley, muttering about trolleys being at a premium. They disappear out of the ward, swearing and grumbling. A nurse sees me sitting on the bed, crying. She explains gently, "We need an X-ray and abdominal scan prior to surgery."

"So I'm not going to surgery today?" It is almost too much to bear. The grumpy-looking porter returns with a wheelchair, still complaining angrily about "nurses requesting trolleys for patients who can walk".

He leaves me in a corridor, alone, my theatre gown gaping at the back. He is muttering something about his rates of pay and the radiologists being paid far too much. He vanishes. I am alone and feeling completely humiliated.

There is nothing like a huge overworked and struggling hospital to remind you of your vulnerability. Money and success count for nothing here. I suddenly feel a little like Danson on his rubbish tip at Eldoret… for a few brief hours, rather than for a lifetime, I feel as if I am nothing in the world and of no value at all. It is a deep and dark lesson in truly identifying with the poor.

Where is God in all this? I don't know.

During my scan, the radiologist asks me if my bowel is blocked. "No, it's an ovarian cyst or appendicitis," I say, faintly.

"Strange. I can't find your ovaries; there is a large dark

shadow showing up…"

Panic!

Back on the ward, my mind is in turmoil. Broken promises and bad behaviour, wrong diagnosis: what's going on? My pain is unbearable, both physical and mental.

John arrives to visit me and I can see from his shocked face that he is very worried: "You're meant to be recovering from surgery now!" I plead with him to take me home.

"I just want to die in my own bed."

Those words may seem overdramatic, but it was exactly how I felt. Emotionally and physically, I thought I was on the edge of life, and just about to fall off into the darkness.

The physical problems were, in the end, relatively easy to sort out. John made contact with the brilliant consultant who had helped him so much, and before long I was diagnosed with a twisted bowel and given excellent treatment. The operation went perfectly well and I was soon on the road to recovery.

Physically sorted, but spiritually…?

That was a different matter. I felt utterly crushed. What made things worse was that I was reacting inside whenever well-meaning Christian friends mentioned church or asked if they could pray with me. I wanted none of it. When I was alone, tears flowed freely and I couldn't see beyond my own misery. To be honest, fear was gripping my heart and I was gradually moving into a state of emotional numbness.

Remember that all this is in the context of the life you have read about, and all the amazing experiences and blessings I have known along the way. I felt cut off from God.

After three weeks like this, I had a visit from my friend Mavis Brewer. We sat in the garden feeling the warm sun on our faces. Mavis began to speak.

"I know how you feel, Rosie; I suffered dreadfully with a painful back. I was angry with God, but eventually I came through it, and you will too."

I looked at her and she could sense the hopelessness that had invaded my spirit, like a freezing fog. She placed her hand on my arm gently.

"Look at what you are achieving through your work in Africa: all those children who need your support; you can't give up on them. There is still so much more that you have to do. I know you don't want me to pray, but I'm going to pray anyway."

I can't recall what I said, but I clearly remember that Mavis was speaking to me like my mum would have done. I felt like a lost child in need of a mother's comfort and understanding. I hugged Mavis tearfully, thanking her for coming. I waved her goodbye and soon took to my bed, exhausted.

As I lay on my bed, I experienced a warmth inside. The icicles around my heart began to melt. I cried out, "God, where were You when I needed You?" But the silence was full of love… God longs to hear from the heart. He wants us to be real about how we are feeling… for a while I was hiding my emotional pain, I was good at pretending. I really struggled trying to cope with my experiences in hospital and old wounds from the past began to surface. I was ashamed of my behaviour and mood swings.

When John asked me what was wrong, I always answered, "I don't know." Eventually I talked to a female doctor who understood exactly what I was going through. She diagnosed anxiety and depression, prescribing medication and recommending a helpful book called *Mind Over Mood* by Dennis Greenberger & Christine A. Padesky. Gradually I began to understand how damaged I had become from experiences beyond my control. My recovery took quite some time – however, I am now back to my old self.

I wanted to share this episode of my life because I am very much aware that, in the UK, a quarter of the population will suffer some kind of mental health problems in the course of a year, with anxiety and depression being the most common mental disorder. It is a silent illness that can lead to a sense of loneliness and isolation.

My home church, St. James, has started a short series of study, based on teaching from the book *The Emotionally Healthy Church* by Peter Scazzero. I was riveted throughout the first session led by Mark Dyer. He started with the Story of Titanic. Built in 1912, more than 1,500 died when the ship hit an iceberg, making it one of the worst sea disasters in history. Icebergs are so dangerous for ships as most of them are under the surface, not seen. I hope to learn more about what lies beneath the surface of our lives in order to understand how to deal with the emotions of my heart and allow Jesus to touch and transform me from within.

I have called this chapter "Full Circle", not only because it is all about returning to roots in Clitheroe but because sometimes, as the poet T. S. Eliot wrote, we need to go back to where we started our journey and "know the place for the first time".

In the months and years that have followed my crisis of faith, the words of St Paul have come back to me:

Who shall separate us from the love of Christ? Shall trouble or hardship or persecution or famine or nakedness or danger or sword? ... No, in all these things we are more than conquerors through him who loved us. For I am convinced that neither death nor life, neither angels nor demons, neither the present nor the future, nor any powers, neither height nor depth, nor anything else in all creation, will be able to separate us from the love of God that is in Christ Jesus our Lord.

Romans 8:35–39 (NIV)

I believe that God does not see people in terms of good and bad, or success and failure, but much more in terms of lost and found.

Sometimes we get lost on the pathway of life, but even through the darkest days and the desert landscapes of our lives, God comes looking for us.

As the old hymn suggests, "Love will never let us go."

Another reason I have talked about the downs as well as the ups is that this brings a great balance and truth to our lives. John and I have had our fair share of good fortune and the last few years have often seemed like a shower of blessings. As we celebrate, we are able to remember those we love and those who are suffering and, through the work of the Foundation, we are able to keep our feet on the ground.

But I have to admit, my two feet nearly took off recently…. At Buckingham Palace!

John has received many honours, including an honorary doctorate from the University of Manchester Institute of Science and Technology. Dr John Lancaster! The boy who left school as a no-hoper, without qualifications! He also received an MBE in Her Majesty's New Year Honours list

Rosemary and John with Maddie and Josh after John received his MBE. Photograph by Charles Green.

in 2011 and we both had an amazing day at Buckingham Palace. But I never expected to be going back to the Palace in my own right.

I have been happy to support John in everything (well, nearly everything!) and to work for the Lancaster Foundation – this is plenty of reward in itself.

I could never have imagined that I would be worthy of an MBE myself. I still don't feel I am, and I have to pinch myself to make sure it has not all been an incredible dream, ever since a phone call from a Palace official to our hotel in Mauritius, where we were staying in November 2015. The well spoken lady was asking politely whether I was prepared to accept the award, since the Palace had not heard back from me. By this time, I had just been alerted by Steven, who had opened the mail at home, but I daren't admit this breach of protocol!

"Award?" I blurted.

"Yes, Mrs Lancaster. You have been awarded the MBE in Her Majesty's New Year Honours." A brief silence. "Are you happy to accept the award?"

"Oh yes… yes… very happy!"

We had already danced round the phone when Steven and Anna, Julie and Philip had all gathered together to ring me. Now I was dancing again, perhaps a little more sedately. "Yes, I would be delighted to accept this…er… great honour…" I almost forgot myself completely and called the lady "Your Majesty".

However, I don't think the Queen would have had the time to ring me personally at my holiday hotel in Mauritius:

"Oh hello, Rose, how are you? And how is John? I believe that my son Charles met him at Buckingham Palace a few years ago. Is he behaving himself? I hear he's quite a handful."

Well, I'd better describe the whole incredible day. William Thackeray, the great Victorian writer, once said, "Good humour is one of the best articles of dress one can wear in society." So I started with that but, you'll be relieved to hear, I did add some other clothes as well.

You bet! I got the dress, the hat, the pearls; the whole package! So, here it is… Hot off the press…

I'm feeling good and full of fun as we leave our hotel at 9.30 a.m. John looks the perfect escort, along with my perfect companions – grand-daughters Erin and Gracie, wearing dusky pink dresses and sparkly headbands. My lovely princesses!

This is the day following Queen Elizabeth's ninetieth birthday celebration, and London is buzzing. My grandchildren soon present me with a mechanical model of Her Majesty, entitled "Dancing Queen"! Our taxi to the Palace is filled with the sound of my adapted version of the ABBA song: "Dancing queen, young and sweet, only *seventy*… You can dance, you can jive, having the time of your life…"

The girls are still giggling as we ascend the Palace steps, up the red carpet. Guards are standing like statues and friendly staff are directing us along the "path of honour"… from here, John and the girls make their way to the ballroom and I join the nervous recipients in the Green Hall.

Clear and precise instructions are given: "Ladies curtsey,

gentlemen bow, then take two steps forward; when the Duke of Cambridge speaks, you must first address him as 'Your Royal Highness', and from then on as 'Sir'. When Prince William offers his hand in farewell, take two steps backwards, curtsey, exit right, trip up, and hurtle backwards down the marble steps, where you will collide with a very large sherry trifle…"

Well, all right, I am slightly elaborating on those final instructions… But my mind is racing with all the possibilities, especially for disaster. I know that the comedian Norman Wisdom tripped up deliberately on receiving his knighthood – and made the Queen laugh – but what if I trip up accidentally? No one will laugh, except John, of course.

The whole event is like a pure fantasy, especially for a girl like me who always dreamed of meeting her Prince Charming… my excitement barometer is about to explode, because now I am going to meet a *real prince*.

The seventy recipients are making their way to the ballroom, where the Countess of Wessex String Orchestra are playing. I glance towards my family, and the girls are waving feverishly. Tears of joy begin to sting my eyes. "Hold it together, Rose," I am whispering to myself.

The moment arrives. My name is announced: "Rosemary Lancaster". Prince William attaches the beautiful ribbon and brooch to my lapel, smiling and saying warmly, "Congratulations!" He is very thoughtful and polite (I suppose he couldn't be rude: "Is that hat yours, or are you wearing it for a bet?"), but he puts me perfectly at my ease. He asks about the Lancaster Foundation, listening intently as I talk about our work in Africa. He is delighted to hear about my visit to Lesotho, saying, "Harry will be happy to hear that." He then wants to know how we raise funds. I happily explain about our successful business and our desire to use our resources to help those less fortunate, saying what a great privilege it is to bless others. Smiling, Prince William shakes my hand and says "Nice to meet you" in a way that makes me truly believe it. I take my two steps back, curtsey, and then, briefly, I break the rules… I can't help myself, but I wink at Prince William.

Luckily, I am not arrested and taken to the Tower: "Twenty-five years for winking without a royal warrant!" Feeling a little foolish, I submerge myself in the crowd and make my exit. Equilibrium is restored as I hug my family.

Leaving Buckingham Palace, we experience a truly regal moment as we proudly walk towards the crowds of sightseers eager to catch a glimpse of a celebrity. We are in such a state of euphoria that we don't realize that the crowds are probably all looking past us to somebody else, much more famous… but what does it matter? My family are there, at the gates, clicking cameras and recording our march of triumph.

During these moments of supreme joy, I suddenly remembered a prophecy prayed over me years previously, when I was feeling rubbish and useless: "One day, Rose, you will speak to kings." Wow… today a future king, and one day, "the King of kings".

Who knows what life still holds for me? For any of us? Whatever happens, good and bad, up and down, I look

Rosemary receives her MBE from Prince William. Image courtesy of British Ceremonial Arts Limited.

forward to the final and greatest Royal Encounter.

Now *that* will be really something!

> *He will wipe every tear from their eyes. There will be no more death or mourning or crying or pain, for the old order of things has passed away.*
>
> *He who was seated on the throne said, "I am making everything new!" Then he said, "Write this down, for these words are trustworthy and true."*
>
> *He said to me, "It is done. I am the Alpha and the Omega, the Beginning and the End. To the thirsty, I will give water without cost from the spring of the water of life."*

Revelation 21:4–6 (NIV)

Rosemary with Gracie and Erin after receiving her MBE.

Reflections from Switzerland

"To understand where you are going, you must understand where you come from."
(Celtic proverb)

Once again, I am sitting in La Bénédiction, Switzerland. It's amazing to think that six years have gone by and I am finally about to write the epilogue for my book. My little songbird still sings in the distance, delighting my senses and warming my heart. "Almost there, almost there!"

I realize that I have been writing this book for myself, my children, my grandchildren, and, I hope, many others across the world. I am truly blessed, remembering what God has done for me throughout my seventy years of life and what a great privilege it is to travel on this deep journey of memory, through so many adventures.

Reflecting in this way has been about the past, but my emotions are all about the future. Every grandparent discovers the future through their grandchildren and the next generation.

As I look back, I see the footprints of a human life being

led by God, a divine pattern, the intricate weaving of a love that is at the centre of the universe.

My story is unfinished; I am unfinished, as God continues to work on my life. I truly believe that "the best is yet to come" and, of course, that God Himself gets to write the final chapter…

La Bénédiction, Switzerland, May 2016

Rosemary and John with their children and grandchildren.

The Lancaster Foundation

My daughter-in-law Anna now works for The Lancaster Foundation. Anna has a deep faith, a kind heart, and a passionate desire to bring out the best in people – this fits perfectly within her role as trust director. Here is what she says:

The Foundation has grown quite considerably in the work that it supports since it began in 1998. It continues to work with charities it has supported from the early days, but has gathered other wonderful partners along the way.

   Currently, there are four main areas of focus for the Foundation's investments:

• Development work overseas, with a particular interest in Africa
• Social action projects in the UK
• Youth projects, with particular emphasis on those with a Christian ethos
• The local community of Clitheroe and surrounding area.

John and Rose have always felt passionately about investing in the arts, the local community, and young people. The creation of The Grand venue in Clitheroe was a perfect mix of all these loves.

There are many charities and causes to which we decide to "scatter" one-off gifts, to help them in their amazing work. This is one of my many privileged roles within the Foundation – I help to research the selected applicants and follow them up in person.

There are so many needs, and it is hard not to respond to all of them, but naturally we have to be very thoughtful and discriminating and to keep focused in all we do. A friend once shared some advice they had been given regarding their work out in Uganda: "Start small and grow up – don't start big and blow up!" I think that this was really wise advice and I always remember this principle when being approached by passionate individuals with big hearts and plans.

Rose's book has told the remarkable story of many of our major partnerships, but I can mention quite a number of other organizations that have benefited in one way or another over the last two years: *Breakout Magazine*, Home-Start, Christian Surfers UK, Youth for Christ, Manchester City Mission, Toybox (working with street children in Guatemala), Street Child in Sierra Leone, Serve Our Community. There are many others, but perhaps this brief list helps to illustrate that we are open-minded and that we try to keep expanding our horizons – even though, of course, there are many requests we cannot meet. Throughout this journey and with this responsibility, I try to remain sensitive, along with my colleagues. We keep listening and learning.

Anna Lancaster, Trust Director

A note from Rosemary:

I am truly grateful for my brilliant team at Lancaster Foundation.

Thank you so much for your enthusiasm and commitment. You are all highly valued and deeply loved.

Rosemary x

Trustees: Rosemary Lancaster MBE, Dr John Lancaster MBE, Steven Lancaster, Julie Broadhurst
Trust Director: Jilly Farthing
Trust Director: Anna Lancaster
Development Director: Chris Richardson
Accounts and Finance: Sue Isherwood

"Everything that God gives us is first a gift to enjoy, then a seed to sow."

– Bob Gass

For your interest and information, you can visit the websites of projects that are dear to my heart. You can read stories of courage from those who are scattering kindness day after day. We are all on a journey, we all have a story to tell that can touch the life of another – God has a plan that includes you, dear reader, your life is precious to him.

Dare to dream; I did…

"Wheresoever you go, go with all your heart."

– Confucius (551–479 BC)

www.message.org.uk

www.saltminetrust.org.uk

www.openarmsinternational.co.uk

www.sparrow.org.za

www.liverpoollighthouse.com

www.maf-uk.org

www.ngm.org.uk

www.thesolomonproject.co.uk

www.capuk.org

www.medair.org

www.tlg.org.uk

www.marysmeals.org.uk

www.thegrandvenue.co.uk

www.revelationlife.org.uk

www.betel.uk

www.biblesociety.org.uk

www.urbansaints.org

www.cinnamonnetwork.co.uk

www.wayfarertrust.org

www.themagdaleneproject

www.ucb.co.uk

www.StJamesclitheroe.co.uk